Published by Smith and Kraus, Inc.
PO Box 127, Lyme, NH 03768

Manufactured in the United States of America
First Edition: March 1998
10 9 8 7 6 5 4 3 2 1
Cover and Text Design by Julia Hill/Freedom Hill Design
Cover Illustration by Aline Ordman

The Library of Congress Cataloging-In-Publication Data
McCullough, L.E.
Plays from mythology: grades 4–6 / L.E. McCullough. —1st ed.
p. cm. — (Young actors series)
Includes bibliographical references.
Summary: Presents twelve original plays that are dramatic adaptations
of myths from around the world.
ISBN 1-57525-110-8
1. Children's plays, American. 2. Mythology—Juvenile drama.
[1. Mythology—Drama. 2. Plays.] I. Title. II. Series.
PS3563.C35297P56   1997
812'.54—dc21   97-32882
CIP
AC

Plays from Mythology
Grades 4–6

L.E. McCullough

YOUNG ACTORS SERIES

SK
A Smith and Kraus book

DEDICATION

This book is dedicated to the Shaman and Scribe of olden times, and to the present-day keeper of humankind's mythic treasures — the Artist.

ontents

Foreword

To grasp the full value of the mythological figures that have come down to us, we must understand that they are not only symptoms of the unconscious (as indeed are all human thoughts and acts) but also controlled and intended statements of certain spiritual principles, which have remained as constant throughout the course of human history as the form and nervous structure of the human physique itself.

— Joseph Campbell,
The Hero with a Thousand Faces

For the playmaker, mythology offers a limitless fund of terrific stories and epic characters that reveal human nature at its core. Mythology is basic to every human social grouping, from tribes to nations, from churchgoers to gang members. In its simplest function, mythology explains the principles of your particular universe and fixes your place within it.

The English word myth is derived from the Greek *mythos,* which originally meant "word" or "story," and it is with the ancient Greek myths that most Americans and Europeans are familiar. Yet, every human culture on the planet has at one time possessed some generative mythology offering a complex "meta-physics" above and beyond Science that details what's really going on in the universe. At the brink of the 21st Century, in our modern world of microbes and microchips, the undercurrent of mythology flows daily through our most common words and thoughts...

Cupid's Bow...Trojan Horse...Noah's Ark...Achilles' Heel...
Golden Fleece...Artist's Muse...even the days of our week —
Tiu's Day, Woden's Day, Thor's Day, Freya's Day, Saturn's Day.

Plays from Mythology have been designed to combine
with studies in other disciplines: history, science, language,
dance, music, social studies — and most suitably for young
students — ethics and psychology of human behavior. *The
Monkey King* can supplement lesson plans in ecology. *King
Midas and the Golden Touch* can generate a pre- or post-
play discussion about precious minerals and ancient metal-
lurgy. *Dreamtime Down Under* is an excellent introduction
to the terrain and wildlife of Australia. Most of the plays are
originally from non-English-speaking peoples; feel free to
have the characters speak a few additional lines of the native
language, and decorate the set with architecture, plants and
art objects specific to that region. If you are a music teacher
and want to add songs and music to any of the plays, go
ahead and make it a class project by organizing a chorus or
having students select appropriate recordings from the host
culture to play before and after the performance.

Besides those children enrolled in the onstage cast, others can be included in the production as lighting and sound
technicians, prop masters, script coaches and stage man-
agers. *Plays from Mythology* is an excellent vehicle for getting other members of the school and community involved
in your project. Maybe there are ethnic dance troupes or
accomplished performers of ethnic music in your area; ask
them to give a special concert or lecture when you present
the play. There are undoubtedly several knowledgeable
scholars at your local historical society, library, art museum,
high school and college who can add interesting tidbits
about the customs and folklore that provide background for
these tales. Try utilizing the talents of local school or youth
orchestra members to play incidental music...get the school
art club to paint scrims and backdrops...see if a senior citi-
zens' group might volunteer time to sew costumes...inquire

whether any local restaurants might bring samples of ethnic cuisine.

Most of all, have lots of fun. Realizing that many performing groups may have limited technical and space resources, I have kept sets, costumes and props minimal. However, if you do have the ability to build an Egyptian pyramid for *The Throne of Osiris* or fashion a facsimile of the Minotaur's Labyrinth for *The Flight of Icarus* — go for it! Adding more music and dance and visual arts and crafts into the production involves more children and makes your play a genuinely multi-media event.

Similarly, I have supplied only basic stage and lighting directions. Blocking is really the province of the director; once you get the play up and moving, feel free to suit cast and action to your available population and experience level of actors. When figuring out how to stage these plays, I suggest you follow the venerable UYI Method — Use Your Imagination. If the play calls for a boat, bring in a wood frame, an old bathtub or have children draw a boat and hang as a scrim behind where the actors perform. Keep in mind the spirit of the old Andy Hardy musicals: "C'mon, everybody! Let's make a show!"

Age and gender. Obviously, your purpose in putting on the play is to entertain as well as educate; even though one typically thinks of castle guards and king's soldiers as being male, there is no reason these roles can't be played in your production by females; likewise for gender-bound Ice Giants, Valkyries and Muses. After all, the essence of the theatrical experience is to suspend us in time and ask us to believe that anything may be possible. Once again, UYI! Adult characters, such as grandparents and "old wise men/women" can certainly be played by children costumed or made up to fit the part as closely as possible, or they can actually be played by adults. While *Plays from Mythology* are intended to be performed chiefly by children, moderate adult involvement will add validation and let children know this isn't just a "kid project." If you want to get very highly choreographed or musically intensive, you will probably find a strategically placed onstage adult or two very helpful in keeping things moving smoothly. Still, never underestimate the capacity for even the youngest children to amaze you with their skill and ingenuity in making a show blossom.

Plays from Mythology is a great way for children to explore ancient history and see the world through the eyes of our ancestors. And for adults, these plays offer a chance to recapture the joy and excitement we all felt the first time we heard the thrilling words "once upon a time..." Who says you can't be a kid again? Just step aboard this magic carpet and follow the big blue genie... mind that dragon lurking round the corner!

L.E. McCullough, Ph.D.
Humanities Theatre Group
Indiana University-Purdue University at Indianapolis
Indianapolis, Indiana

A Note on Costumes, Sets and Music

Most myths are set in a "legendary time" that most closely corresponds in real cultural and costume details to the centuries before Christ, c. 500-2500 B.C. For plays set in specific countries, books on ethnic dress can be consulted as well. Dover Books publishes several good collections of period costumes, two of which are:

- *What People Wore: A Visual History of Dress from Ancient Times to 20th-Century America.* Douglas Gorsline. This has a huge bibliography of other costume books.

- *Historic Costume in Pictures.* Braun & Schneider. New York, NY: Dover Books.

To decorate your scrims and background sets, Dover also publishes iron-on transfer books of gargoyles and folklore creatures, angels, wild animals — plus calligraphy, floral patterns and ornamental designs from cultures around the world including African, Asian, Celtic, American Indian, Old European and more.

If you'd like some costuming ideas for gods, goddesses, heroes and other mythic characters, check out these books:

- *World Mythology.* Roy Willis, editor. New York, NY: Henry Holt and Co.

- *The Dictionary of World Myth.* Peter Bentley, editor. New York, NY: Facts on File.

- *Gods and Mortals in Classical Mythology.* Michael Grant and John Hazel. Springfield, MA: G. & C. Merriam Co.

- *The Illustrated Who's Who in Mythology.* Michael Senior. New York, NY: MacMillan.

Using authentic ethnic or period music is a great way to enhance your production. The public library is always a good source, yet recordings of folk and ethnic international music are increasingly available at mainstream record stores and from catalogues. If you have questions about where to find recordings or written music of the tunes or genres included in these plays, or want some tips on performing and arranging them, I would be happy to assist you and may be reached by email at Feadaniste@AOL.COM.

Plays from Mythology

Grades 4–6

Dreamtime Down Under

Perhaps the oldest surviving mythology in the world is that of the Aboriginal people of Australia. Aborigines (who call themselves *Kurri* — meaning "our people") have been in Australia for close to 60,000 years and illustrate their myths in paintings on rock, sand and bark; some of these paintings surviving today were made nearly 30,000 years ago. Central to Aboriginal mythology is the "Dream Time," an ancient time when the ancestors travelled across Australia shaping the landscape, structuring society and depositing the spirits of unborn children in animals, trees and people. It is believed that the energy of an ancient being can be released by rubbing or striking the place where he or she left the world; anyone born at that site, becomes a guardian of that spirit.

RUNNING TIME: 20 minutes

PLACE: Australia

CAST: 19 actors, min. 4 boys (•), 2 girls (+)

• Jim Borala the Song Man	4 People
+ Naarit the Cockatoo	• Lakemaker
• Hunter	+ Murgah Muggui
• Mullyan	Crow
Koala	Kangaroo
Goanna (Lizard)	Gur-Gur (Sparrowhawk)
Mopoke (Owl)	Emu
Wombat	Kookaburra (Kingfisher)

STAGE SET: rock at down right; three other rocks at mid center

PROPS: 2 pair of wooden sticks (app. 10-12 inches in length), boomerang, 4 duck masks, 2 spears, small dilly-bag (neck-bag), *didjeridoo* (straight wooden trumpet, 4-5 feet in length; a tinwhistle, recorder or flute can substitute, but try making your own *didjeridoo*!)

EFFECTS: sound — thunder and lightning

MUSIC: *Corroboree of Naarit*; *Corroboree of Crow*; *In the Dream Time*

COSTUMES: Characters wear Aboriginal traditional costume, accented by feathers on head and in armbands and legbands, white stripes painted on arms, legs and face; Murgah Muggui wears a black shawl; Animals wear appropriate masks and coverings; Crow first appears not in black but in beige or tan colors, then black

PRONUNCIATION:
   bugeen — bu-**geen'**
   corroboree— cor-o-**bor'**-ee
   didjeridoo — dij-er-ee-**doo'**
   kuran — **koo'**-ran
   Mopoke — Mo-**po'**-ke
   Murgah Muggui — Mur-ga **Mu'**-gee
   Mullyan — **Mull'**-yan
   Naarit — **Na'**-rit
   wirreenun — wir-**ee'**-nun

(LIGHTS UP RIGHT ON JIM BORALA sitting on rock at down right; he holds a didjeridoo and blows a few low sustained notes.)

JIM BORALA: *(to audience)* My name is Jim Borala, and I live in the bush country of Australia. They call me the Song Man because I play the *didjeridoo*, possibly the oldest musical instrument in the world. When did people start making music, you ask? Well, it was back in the Dream Time, thousands and thousands and thousands of years ago.

(LIGHTS UP CENTER ON FOUR PEOPLE lying on the ground at mid center or propped up against rocks, sleeping.)

JIM BORALA: It was shortly after Uli-tarra, the Supreme Being, had finished making the world. Or almost finished, because there were a few things missing — like music for the People.

(NAARIT THE COCKATOO enters from left and perches on the rock at left mid center; she squawks and chatters in a high, piping voice as the People awake.)

PERSON #1: Look, it is a white cockatoo! Listen to her yabber!
PERSON #2: Why is it making those strange noises?
PERSON #3: I have heard other animals doing that. They call it "singing a song"!
PERSON #4: I bet I can catch that song!

(Person #4 creeps behind Naarit the Cockatoo and grabs her, pinning back her arms.)

PERSON #1: She will make a fine bit of tucker!

NAARIT THE COCKATOO: Oh, please, please! Do not eat me!

PERSON #2: And why not?

NAARIT THE COCKATOO: Because I am Naarit, a noble cockatoo!

PERSON #3: And what makes you so noble?

NAARIT THE COCKATOO: I have a song taught to me by Uli-tarra, Maker of the World.

PERSON #4: Then you must give us that song! We are creatures of Uli-tarra, too!

NAARIT THE COCKATOO: Very well. We will make a *corroboree*, and you shall sing the song of Naarit the Cockatoo!

(Naarit the Cockatoo flutters to down center, with the People behind him; Persons #1 and 2 each pick up a pair of sticks from ground.)

JIM BORALA: Naarit taught the People how to make the *didjeridoo* and how to play sticks and bones. Then she taught them to dance and sing a *corroboree*.

(Persons #3 and 4 dance to music as Persons #1 and 2 beat rhythm with sticks. MUSIC: "Corroboree of Naarit.")

NAARIT THE COCKATOO: *(sings)*
The cockatoo lives in the hot desert.
Where can she find water?

NAARIT THE COCKATOO & FOUR PEOPLE: *(sing)*
Allo-allo, burra-burra, bo-bo!

NAARIT THE COCKATOO: *(sings)*
Naarit will show you the water
That lives in the heart of the ironwood tree.

NAARIT THE COCKATOO & FOUR PEOPLE: *(sing)*
Allo-allo, burra-burra, bo-bo!

(Dance and music stops; Naarit the Cockatoo flutters offstage left.)

PERSON #1: The "Corroboree of Naarit" is a good song!
PERSON #2: It tells us where *we* can find water, too!
PERSON #3: We must always sing this song—
PERSON #4: So we do not forget how to live in the desert.

(Four People exit left, dancing.)

JIM BORALA: And to this day, the Kurri — that is what we original people of Australia call ourselves — sing this song and many others like it. All the songs of a tribe form a "songline." And each songline is a map that tells you where you are on your journey through life. This is how the world was formed, you see — by the journeys of our ancestors!

(LAKEMAKER enters from left, carrying a boomerang; he stops at down left and looks across stage toward mid right.)

JIM BORALA: Once back in the Dream Time there was a man on a walkabout in the desert. And very soon, he became lost.
LAKEMAKER: Sand, nothing but sand as far as the eye can see!
JIM BORALA: So he called upon his *kuran* — his own personal spirit that lived inside him!
LAKEMAKER: You have the power to shape your own world!
JIM BORALA: And he threw his boomerang at the far horizon!

(Lakemaker mimes throwing boomerang across stage.)

JIM BORALA: It tore a huge wedge in the earth! And, so the man threw it again! And again! And again!

(Lakemaker mimes throwing boomerang across stage several times.)

JIM BORALA: Until he had carved out a giant hole in the desert and formed many large mountains with the sand thrown up around it. And when the rains came—

(LIGHTS FLICKER QUICKLY ON AND OFF; SOUND: THUNDER AND LIGHTNING OFFSTAGE as Lakemaker dances to mid center, arms raised to the sky.)

JIM BORALA: The water flowed into the hole and formed Lake Nabberu! Oh, but the mighty Lakemaker was not finished with his creating!

(Lakemaker sits on rock at mid center; Four People enter from left and stand at down left looking toward Lakemaker.)

JIM BORALA: As he sat at the edge of the lake, he saw a band of strange men coming toward him.
LAKEMAKER: It is the *bugeen* — spirits of the desert who are angry at me for changing their land!

(Lakemaker mimes throwing boomerang at Four People; they mime getting hit in chin and pull up duck masks over their faces.)

JIM BORALA: So Lakemaker threw his boomerang at the *bugeen*! And he struck each one in the chin, cutting out a piece from their beards!
LAKEMAKER: When this happened, the *bugeen* changed from men into musk ducks and swam out into the water

of the lake. This is why musk ducks today have a pouch that looks like a man's chipped beard.

(Four People exit left, quacking, as Lakemaker heads to right exit, stopping at down right and addressing audience.)

LAKEMAKER: In the Dream Time, all the animals, all the birds, all the reptiles — even the sun, moon and stars could talk to each other the way People do now. Because we all shared the same dreams. *(exits)*

JIM BORALA: You do not think so? Well, here is another story that proves it!

(MURGAH MUGGUI enters from left, creeping to a rock at mid center; A HUNTER enters from right, carrying a spear and looking out toward the audience.)

JIM BORALA: There once was a terrible old *wirreenun* — a witch — who lived by herself in the bush. Her name was Murgah Muggui, and not only was she a witch, she was a bloodthirsty *bunna* — a cannibal! When she saw a young man fossicking about by the billabong, she would change herself into a beautiful young woman.

(Murgah Muggui puts shawl over her face and, as Hunter nears, pulls it away and gestures to him, smiling.)

MURGAH MUGGUI: My dear young hunter! It is late, and I am alone in the bush! Will you not camp with me tonight?

HUNTER: I am very hungry and far from home.

MURGAH MUGGUI: Let me make you something to eat. How about some nice cackleberries and rock melon?

(Hunter sits and relaxes against rock, falling asleep, as Murgah Muggui mimes kneading bread.)

JIM BORALA: After the meal, the hunter would fall asleep. And Murgah Muggui would strike! And have *her* meal!

(Murgah Muggui stabs Hunter in heart with his spear, then drags him behind rock; MULLYAN enters from left, carrying a spear and looking out toward the audience.)

JIM BORALA: One day not long after, a man named Mullyan came into the bush hunting. Mullyan was very brave. And very clever. As night began to fall, he came to the billabong and met a beautiful young woman who offered to let him stay at her camp.

(Murgah Muggui welcomes Mullyan and has him sit against the rock.)

MURGAH MUGGUI: You look positively knackered! Rest, and I will make you a very special meal!

(Murgah Muggui mimes kneading bread as Mullyan falls asleep.)

JIM BORALA: And when she thought Mullyan was asleep, she made her move.

(Murgah Muggui reaches for Mullyan's spear, but he grabs it, jumps up and stabs her in the stomach.)

MULLYAN: You will not feed on human flesh ever again, cursed *wirreenun*!

(With the spear still in her stomach, Mullyan drives Murgah Muggui offstage left.)

JIM BORALA: And the evil witch died, but her spirit turned into — you guessed it — the spider, who every hour of the day spins pretty webs to catch her insect victims.

(KOALA, GOANNA, MOPOKE, EMU, WOMBAT, GUR-GUR, KANGAROO and KOOKABURRA enter from right, dancing to down center as instrumental music plays. CROW, wearing a small bag around his neck, enters from left, strutting and ignoring the others who form around him. MUSIC: "Corroboree of Crow.")

KOALA: Long ago none of the animals had fire. Not I, Koala.
GOANNA: Nor I, Goanna the Lizard.
WOMBAT: Nor I, Wombat.
MOPOKE: Nor I, Mopoke the Owl.
EMU: Nor I, Emu.
GUR-GUR: Nor I, Gur-Gur the Sparrowhawk.
KANGAROO: Nor I, Kangaroo.
KOOKABURRA: Nor I, Kookaburra the Kingfisher.
KOALA: None of us have fire.
GOANNA: Except for one.
WOMBAT, MOPOKE & EMU: Crow!
GUR-GUR, KANGAROO & KOOKABURRA: Crow!
CROW: Fire? Not I?
WOMBAT, MOPOKE & EMU: Liar!
GUR-GUR, KANGAROO & KOOKABURRA: Liar!
CROW: Call me liar, but I have no fire!
KOALA: When *we* eat, *our* faces show the traces of our uncooked meal.
GOANNA: Yet the color red is never seen about *your* face, Crow.
CROW: I take very tiny bites. And I use a napkin! You should try it sometime!

(Animals move away from Crow, who cautiously fon-

dles the dillybag around his neck; Animals talk among themselves.)

KOALA: Look at that old dobber, acting like he's never even *heard* of fire!

GOANNA: Coming the raw prawn with his mates! Crow's no fair dinkum!

KANGAROO: Always slinging off about his bickies!

GUR-GUR: And giving us curry about our table manners!

WOMBAT: Somebody needs to sort that smooger out!

MOPOKE: Spot on! Let's nick his swag!

EMU: Why don't we just have a sticky in that dillybag hanging round his scrawny neck?

KOOKABURRA: And get the dinky di on where Crow keeps fire!

(Animals circle around Crow and begin dancing to music — Goanna, Gur-Gur, Kangaroo and Kookaburra dance while Koala, Wombat, Mopoke and Emu sing and clap. MUSIC: "Corroboree of Crow.")

CROW: Why, how wonderful! The animals are making a *corroboree* for me!

KOALA, WOMBAT, MOPOKE & EMU: *(sing)*
Fire, we call your name!
We ask you to come to us
From whatever hidden place you live!
Allo-allo, burra-burra, bo-bo!

(Gur-Gur comes up behind Crow and grabs his dillybag; Crow chases Gur-Gur around the stage, ending up at down left, where Crow tries to stamp out the fire that has escaped and is spreading on the ground.)

WOMBAT: Gur-Gur has taken Crow's dillybag!

MOPOKE: And, look! Fire is spilling out! Crow kept fire hidden in his dillybag!

EMU: Fire is spreading all over the ground!

KANGAROO: It is setting leaves and grass alight through the bush!

CROW: Come back, fire! Come back to me!

(Crow gets down full-length on ground and rolls around as other Animals laugh and shout.)

KOOKABURRA: Look at Crow trying to put out fire!

GOANNA: Fire will never come back to you, Crow! It belongs to all of us now!

GUR-GUR: Look how black Crow has become by rolling in the burnt grass!

(Crow rolls offstage left, followed by other animals.)

JIM BORALA: And not only did Crow's feathers turn to black, but he got white circles around his eyes where the fire scorched the skin! *(laughs)* Oh, there are many more stories in my songline, all from the Dream Time. Stories about the Rainbow Snake and the Water Lubra, the Seven Sisters and their suitor Karambal, and the story of how the Great Creator made two men out of clay and then cut them into little pieces and scattered them all over the world with a big willy-willy. *(points skyward)* Do you see the stars? Those are where the good men and women landed and look down upon us today! In the Dream Time!

(Jim Borala begins playing the didjeridoo. Entire Cast comes onstage and sings. MUSIC: "In the Dream Time.")

ENTIRE CAST: *(sing)*
    Life is a songline stretching forever
    In the Dream Time!
    Follow the songs to wisdom and knowledge
    In the Dream Time!

    Heroes and tricksters shaping the Earth
    In the Dream Time!
    Animals talking with voices of spirits
    In the Dream Time!

    Ancestor songlines guiding our journey
    In the Dream Time!
    Life is a songline stretching forever
    In the Dream Time!

(LIGHTS OUT.)

THE END

Corroboree of Naarit
(by L.E. McCullough)

♩ = 110

The cock-a-too lives in the hot de-sert. Where can she find wa-ter? Al-lo-al-lo, bur-ra-bur-ra, bo-bo! Naa-rit will show you the wa-ter that lives in the heart of the i-ron-wood tree. Al-lo-al-lo, bur-ra-bur-ra, bo-bo!

Corroboree of Crow
(by L.E. McCullough)

♩ = 140

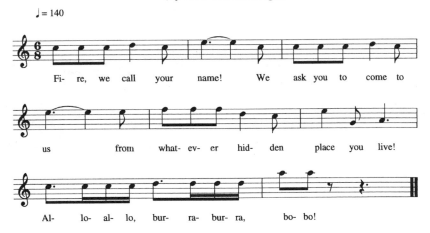

Fi-re, we call your name! We ask you to come to us from what-ev-er hid-den place you live! Al-lo-al-lo, bur-ra-bur-ra, bo-bo!

In the Dream Time
(by L.E. McCullough)

In the Dream Time, pg. 2

Dream Time! Dream Time! An- ces- tor song- lines

Dream Time! Dream Time!

guid- ing our jour-ney in the Dream Time! Dream Time!

Dream Time! Ah- ah-

Life is a song- line stretch- ing for- e- ver in the Dream Time!

ah — ah — ah- ah —

Dream Time! Dream Time! ah- ah- ah!

ah- ah — ah- ah- ah- ah- ah!

Fionn in Search of His Youth

Many ancient Irish myths tell of super-heroes like Fionn mac Cumhaill and the Fianna, a band of warrior adventurers with special powers who battle other warriors and creatures from the spirit world. Stories about Fionn and the Fianna began to be written down in the eighth century A.D., but scholars think that these tales are based on an earlier version of Fionn related to the Celtic sun god Lugh, who was worshipped across Central Europe in the centuries before Christ. Many statues and pictures of Fionn show him sucking his thumb. According to myth, as a boy Fionn was given the job of watching the Salmon of Knowledge while it cooked on a fire. Touching the fish, he burned his thumb and stuck it in his mouth. He was instantly granted the gift of prophecy and would suck his thumb whenever he wanted to predict the future.

RUNNING TIME: 15 minutes

PLACE: Ireland

CAST: 9 actors, min. 5 boys (•), 2 girls (+)

Narrator	• Fionn mac Cumhaill
• Diarmaid	• Oscar
• Conán	• Oisín
+ Young Woman	+ Old Woman
Sheep	

STAGE SET: stool at down right; stool at mid center; table and 4 stools at down left

PROPS: spear, 4 swords, 5 dinner plates, short piece of rope

MUSIC: *Warriors of Tara*

COSTUMES: Fionn and Fianna wear medieval warrior garb
— Fionn carries a spear, Diarmaid, Oscar, Conán and
Oisín each carry a sword or dagger in a belt; Old Woman
and Young Woman wear simple peasant dress — blouse,
skirt, simple shoes or sandals; Sheep wears mask and
wooly body covering; Narrator wears modern clothes,
perhaps an Aran sweater or fisherman's cap

PRONUNCIATION:
  amadán — am-a-**don'**
  Conán — Ko-**non'**
  Diarmaid — **Dyar'**-mud
  Erin go bragh — E-rin go **bra'**
  Fianna — **Fee'**-a-na
  Fionn mac Cumhaill — Fin mac **Koo'**-al
  Gráinne — **Grawn'**-ya
  Niamh — **Nee'**-uv
  Oisín — Ush-**cen'**
  Oscar — **Os'**-ker
  Tir nan Óg — Tir nan **Oag'**
  Tuatha de Danaan — **Too'**-a day **Da'**-non

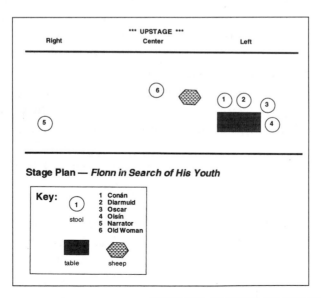

Stage Plan — *Fionn in Search of His Youth*

Key:
  stool
  1 Conán
  2 Diarmuid
  3 Oscar
  4 Oisín
  5 Narrator
  6 Old Woman
  table   sheep

(LIGHTS UP RIGHT ON NARRATOR sitting on stool at down right.)

NARRATOR: *(to audience)* Is it a good myth you're looking for? In this part of Ireland we have plenty. Why, the myths hereabout are thick as feathers on a duck!

(LIGHTS UP CENTER AND LEFT ON FIONN MAC CUMHAILL, DIARMAID, OSCAR, CONÁN and OISÍN marching in from left as MUSIC PLAYS OFFSTAGE; they stride to down center and line up facing audience, stepping forward as their names are called. MUSIC: "Warriors of Tara.")

NARRATOR: One fine day, and not long ago it was, the hero Fionn mac Cumhaill and four of his merry Fianna were out on a hunt in the valley just below. What a mighty band of warriors they were! There was Diarmaid, the noble and fair. There was Oisín, the greatest poet of his age. And his son, Oscar, the fiercest fighter of the band. And Conán, who Fionn had converted from an outlaw, to serve bravely in the cause of justice and the High King of Tara. And, of course, there was the leader of the Fianna — Fionn mac Cumhail himself, who was descended from the majestic race of warrior gods called the Tuatha de Danaan. Fionn possessed a magic spear with a head of bronze and rivets of Arabian gold. When he put the blade of this spear against his forehead, he was filled with a strength that made him invincible in every battle!

(Fionn and the Fianna raise their weapons in the air and cheer.)

FIONN & THE FIANNA: Erin go bragh! Ireland forever!

NARRATOR: Now, Fionn and the lads had spent the entire

day hunting, but they had met no game. Night was falling, and they were tired and a wee bit cranky.

OSCAR: Oh, but there is a powerful thirst upon me!

OISÍN: And the hunger is nipping at my heels like a quarrelsome hound!

DIARMAID: I curse this blasted fog that has us surrounded!

CONÁN: It is a fairy fog and means us no good!

FIONN: *(points to down left)* By the beard of St. Patrick, I see a small cottage yonder! Perchance, it will have the makings of a meal and a place to sleep! To the cottage!

THE FIANNA: To the cottage!

(Fionn and the Fianna march up right and back to down center and then down left as MUSIC PLAYS OFF-STAGE; MUSIC: "Warriors of Tara." OLD WOMAN and SHEEP enter from left; Old Woman sits huddled on stool at mid center and Sheep kneels down between table and Old Woman. The Fianna peer into the cottage.)

OSCAR: It is a *very* small cottage.

OISÍN: And greatly dark and bare.

DIARMAID: There is only an old woman by the hearth.

CONÁN: And a sheep by an empty table. We won't get much to eat here.

FIONN: It is a curious sort of cottage, altogether. Let us enter and be on our guard against sorcery!

OLD WOMAN: You are welcome, strangers, to this house! Sit down at the table and make way for your supper!

(The Fianna sit at the table; Fionn stands to the table's right; YOUNG WOMAN enters from left carrying five dinner plates, which she sets before Fionn and the Fianna.)

OSCAR: This is a grand feast!

OISÍN: Aye! Hunger is a good sauce!

DIARMAID: The seeking for one thing will find another!
CONÁN: The more you get of what's good, the less you'll get of what's bad!

(Fianna mime eating as Sheep rises and crawls under table, then bucks up and upsets table so that plates fall on floor; Sheep crawls back to original spot.)

FIONN: The devil take your wooly back! Our dinner is in smithereens! Conán, get up and tie the sheep to the wall!

(Conán crosses to Sheep and tries to drag it to the right; Sheep does not budge.)

CONÁN: By the great stone of Tara, I cannot move this sheep an inch!
FIONN: Get up, Diarmaid, and tie the sheep!

(Conán returns to table as Diarmaid crosses to Sheep and tries to drag it to the right; Sheep does not budge.)

DIARMAID: If this be a sheep, it must have a boulder in its belly!
OSCAR: An empty pail makes the most noise! *I'll* tie this sheep!

(Diarmaid returns to table as Oscar crosses to Sheep and tries to drag it to the right; Sheep does not budge.)

OISÍN: Stand aside, amadán! Let a man do a man's job!

(Oscar returns to table as Oisín crosses to Sheep and tries to drag it to the right; Sheep does not budge. Oisín returns to table as Fionn puts the blade of his spear against his forehead, holding it there for several seconds.)

CONÁN: Fionn is calling upon his magic spear!

DIARMAID: If it makes him invincible in battle, it will surely help him move the sheep!

(Fionn hands spear to Young Woman, crosses to Sheep and tries to drag it to the right; Sheep does not budge.)

OLD WOMAN: My shame be upon you! The greatest warriors in all Ireland, and you can't tie a sheep to the wall!

(Old Woman rises slowly, hobbles over to Sheep and puts a rope around Sheep's neck, tugging Sheep to her stool with ease, then sitting back down on the stool.)

OSCAR: This is sorcery! The old woman is a witch!

OISÍN: *(draws sword)* Prepare to fight for your lives!

FIONN: *(to Young Woman)* What manner of mischief is this? Who are you, and why have you brought us to this cottage?

YOUNG WOMAN: Ah, Fionn mac Cumhail, do you not know me? *(steps up to him, hands back his spear)* You had me once, but you'll never have me again!

FIONN: *(stares at her)* Know you? I've never seen your face in my life!

YOUNG WOMAN: And you, Conán? Do you not know who I am? And you, Diarmaid? Oscar? Oisín? You had me once, but you'll never have me again!

FIONN: *(brandishes spear)* Cease your riddles, woman, and tell us your mind!

YOUNG WOMAN: Fionn mac Cumhail, that sheep is not of the usual kind. It is Strength. And that old woman by the hearth. She is Death. As strong as the sheep was, the old woman easily overcame her. Death will overcome each of you in the same way, strong as you all may be.

FIONN: And you. Who are you?

YOUNG WOMAN: I am Youth. Each of you once possessed

me, but you never will again. Now, it is within my power to grant you all one wish before you leave.

OSCAR: I wish for a spear that will never miss its mark!

CONÁN: I wish for the power of killing hundreds in battle!

DIARMAID: I wish for a charm to make women fall in love with me!

OISÍN: I wish for the grace of God when it comes my time to die!

YOUNG WOMAN: And you, Fionn mac Cumhail — for what do you wish?

FIONN: Since I can never again possess my Youth, I wish my name to be forever remembered in song and poem, for as long as there are voices to sing and tongues to speak.

YOUNG WOMAN: A wise choice, Fionn mac Cumhail. All of your wishes are granted. Go, and return to Tara. More adventures await you!

(LIGHTS FLICKER ON AND OFF as Sheep, Old Woman and Young Woman exit left; Fionn and the Fianna march to down center and line up facing audience, stepping forward as their names are called.)

NARRATOR: *(to audience)* And it's many adventures they did have. Oscar's spear never missed its mark. Conán was granted the power of killing hundreds — though he had such a bad temper, the other Fianna never told him how the power worked. Diarmaid made a woman named Gráinne fall in love with him, which led to his death by a wild pig. Oisín journeyed to Tir nan Óg and lived for three hundred years with the fairy princess Niamh. And Fionn mac Cumhail — well, it's two thousand years since he left the enchanted cottage, and we're still telling his stories, aren't we?

(Fionn and the Fianna raise their weapons in the air and cheer.)

FIONN & THE FIANNA: Erin go bragh!

(LIGHTS OUT. MUSIC PLAYS OFFSTAGE. MUSIC: "Warriors of Tara.")

THE END

Warriors of Tara
(by T.H. Gillespie)

© T.H. Gillespie 1994

The Flight of Icarus

This tale is from ancient Greek mythology and was first written down in the eighth century B.C. by a farmer named Hesiod, who was also a *rhapsode*, or professional reciter of poetry. Hesiod's most famous work was *Theogony*, a long poem about the creation of the universe and the gods in which many of the myths we know today were set down. The Greeks believed their lives were determined by the interaction of several deities, and every city in Greece had its own set of gods and goddesses. In ancient Greek theatre, the *chorus* did not sing but stood onstage during the play and commented on the action. Actors wore masks that identified the role they played, and the masks had large openings at the mouth that amplified the actor's voice.

RUNNING TIME: 20 minutes

PLACE: Crete

CAST: 19 actors, min. 11 boys (•), 3 girls (+)

• Hesiod	4 Chorus Members
• Daedalus	• Icarus
• King Minos	• Poseidon
Servant	• Theseus
+ Ariadne	• Minotaur
• Atlas	• Hermes
• Prometheus	• Ares
+ Artemis	+ Eagle

STAGE SET: 4' x 4' x 1' riser at mid center

PROPS: trident; 2 swords; small statue of a bull; parchment scroll, with scroll having design of Labyrinth; ball of twine; two sets of wings; large globe of the world; hunting bow

EFFECTS: sound — thunder; visual — lights flicker on and off to simulate lightning

COSTUMES: characters wear ancient Grecian garb — togas and sandals, with headbands for women; Minotaur has a grotesque bull head; Eagle has appropriate mask and wings; the various deities can have items characteristic to their myth

PRONUNCIATION:
Aegeus — **A-gee'**-us
Hesiod — **Hes'**-ee-od
Ares — **Ayr'**-ees
Ariadne — A-ree-**ad'**-nee
Minos — **Mee'**-nos
Dionysius — Dy-o-**nee'**-see-us
Artemis — **Ar'**-te-mis
Minotaur — **Mee'**-no-tar
Poseidon — Po-**sy'**-don
Daedalus — **Da'**-da-lus
Atlas — **At'**-las
Prometheus — Pro-**mee'**-thee-us
Theseus — **Thes'**-ee-us
Hermes — **Her'**-mees
Icarus — **Ik'**-a-rus

(LIGHTS UP FULL on HESIOD standing at down right, FOUR CHORUS MEMBERS standing on riser at mid center; Hesiod addresses audience.)

HESIOD: I am Hesiod the Greek, a simple farmer and keeper of the great myths of our people. It is by these myths that the gods and goddesses who rule the universe allow us mortals to partake of their wisdom and improve our lives on this earth.

CHORUS MEMBERS: Mighty Zeus be praised!

HESIOD: *(points to Chorus)* They are the Chorus, who will help this tale unfold, for it is a tale of great sorrow—

CHORUS MEMBERS: A tragedy in honor of Dionysius, god of ecstatic joy and savage brutality.

HESIOD: And yet also a tale celebrating the heights of genius to which Man can soar!

CHORUS MEMBERS: A comedy befitting bright Apollo, god of truth and beauty.

HESIOD: And thus it was, a very long time ago, there lived a King who ruled the island of Crete.

(KING MINOS enters from right and crosses to down center; POSEIDON, holding trident, enters from left and stands at down left.)

CHORUS MEMBER #1: The King's name was Minos, and he was a very proud King.

CHORUS MEMBER #2: One day he prayed to the god Poseidon, ruler of the sea, asking him for a favor.

KING MINOS: *(arms outstretched, addresses audience)* O Poseidon, whose golden chariot glides across the ocean's white-capped waves, let the people of Crete prosper and dominate the seas of the world!

Hear me, and I shall make a great sacrifice in your honor!

(Poseidon raises trident and strikes the air. SOUND:

THUNDER as LIGHTS FLICKER ON AND OFF; SER-VANT, carrying small statue of a bull, enters from left and presents statue to King Minos at center.)

CHORUS MEMBER #3: Poseidon agreed and sent Minos a bull for the sacrifice.
CHORUS MEMBER #4: But Minos thought the bull so beautiful, he refused to kill it.
POSEIDON: This mortal dares to keep what belongs to a god!

(Poseidon strikes air with trident. SOUND: THUNDER as LIGHTS FLICKER ON AND OFF; Servant exits left with statue and MINOTAUR enters from right, rushing in a frenzy to center where he kneels and moans.)

CHORUS MEMBER #1: Poseidon became very angry and vowed to punish the arrogant King—
CHORUS MEMBER #2: By turning his next-born son into a Minotaur—
CHORUS MEMBER #3: A hideous beast that was half man and half raging bull!
CHORUS MEMBERS: *(scream)* Aiiieeee!

(King Minos raises sword over kneeling, cringing Minotaur.)

CHORUS MEMBER #4: At first the King planned to kill this pathetic creature.
KING MINOS: Mighty Zeus, your brother Poseidon has wrought a foul curse upon my blood! *(lowers sword)* But this creature *is* my blood, and I shall not kill him. Instead, he shall make the name of Minos and the island of Crete known the world over!

(King Minos points sword at mid left; Minotaur rises and slouches to mid left and kneels, facing audience.)

CHORUS MEMBER #1: Minos spared the Minotaur and ordered a special home built for the beast.

CHORUS MEMBER #2: He called to the palace a great architect, named Daedalus.

(DAEDALUS, holding a parchment scroll, enters from right and meets King Minos at down center.)

CHORUS MEMBER #3: And Daedalus built the Labyrinth, a maze of twisting, turning hallways from which escape was impossible.

CHORUS MEMBERS: Impossible!

(Daedalus unrolls scroll and shows its design to King Minos, who nods approvingly; Daedalus crosses to mid right.)

CHORUS MEMBER #4: This was where the Minotaur was kept, confined like a monster.

CHORUS MEMBERS: Monster!

MINOTAUR: *(groans loudly)* Aaarruggggh!

HESIOD: And thus King Minos began to exact his revenge.

KING MINOS: *(raises sword, addresses audience)* Poseidon wishes a sacrifice? Well then, every year, I will offer a tribute — seven young men and seven young maidens taken from our neighboring kingdoms. They will enter the Labyrinth to face the Minotaur.

MINOTAUR: *(rises, roars)* Aaarruggggh!

KING MINOS: And meet their final doom! *(laughs evilly, crosses to down left)*

(THESEUS enters from left and stands at down center,

facing audience; ARIADNE enters from right and gazes longingly upon Theseus as he speaks.)

CHORUS MEMBER #1: When it was time again for the sacrifice, a youth from Athens volunteered to enter the Labyrinth and face the Minotaur.

CHORUS MEMBER #2: His name was Theseus, son of King Aegeus and cousin to Hercules.

THESEUS: My cousin Hercules has no sole claim to feats of greatness. I come to Crete not as victim, but as conqueror. I will slay the Minotaur, and free our people of this curse!

CHORUS MEMBER #3: Ariadne, daughter of Minos, saw fair Theseus and fell in love with him.

ARIADNE: Theseus must not die!

(Ariadne crosses to Daedalus.)

CHORUS MEMBER #4: She sought Daedalus and begged his aid.

ARIADNE: You built the Labyrinth. Surely, there must be a way to escape!

(Daedalus hands her a ball of twine.)

DAEDALUS: Take this ball of twine and give it to your friend. Tell him to fasten it to the inside of the door and unwind it as he walks through the Labyrinth. This way he can retrace his steps and find the way out.

(Ariadne runs to Theseus, hands him ball of twine and runs back to mid right; Theseus takes twine and turns to up left, stealthily approaching Minotaur, who is kneeling.)

CHORUS MEMBER #1: Theseus entered the Labyrinth, trailing the twine behind him as he crept through the maze.

CHORUS MEMBER #2: Finally, he came upon the Minotaur, and surprised him!

(Theseus and Minotaur struggle; Theseus wins and Minotaur falls dead.)

CHORUS MEMBERS: *(cheer)* The Minotaur is dead! Theseus has won! The Minotaur is dead! Theseus has won!

THESEUS: *(raises his arms skyward)* Thanks be to the goddess Pallas Athena, daughter of Zeus and protector of Athens!

(Theseus and Ariadne meet at center, embrace and exit right; Servant enters from left and drags dead Minotaur offstage left; King Minos, enraged, steps to down center and gestures with his sword for Daedalus to meet him; Daedalus timidly crosses to down center, kneeling before King Minos.)

HESIOD: But our tale does not end here. For King Minos, the thirst for vengeance was still unslaked.

KING MINOS: You are a clever man, Daedalus. It was you who gave aid to Theseus and caused the Minotaur to die. Now you shall spend the rest of your life in the Labyrinth! And you will have no ball of twine to effect your escape! *(exits right)*

(Servant enters from left pushing a reluctant ICARUS ahead of him to down center; Icarus takes scroll from Daedalus and studies it as Servant exits left.)

CHORUS MEMBER #3: Imprisoned with Daedalus was his son, Icarus.

CHORUS MEMBER #4: Icarus was a brave youth and well-tutored in the arts of woodcraft and forging.

CHORUS MEMBER #1: But he was impulsive and often spoke rashly before he thought.

ICARUS: *(shows scroll)* Father, it is hopeless! We are doomed to rot and die in this Labyrinth! Even you, who designed this maze, cannot find the way to walk out of here!

DAEDALUS: You are quite correct, my son. We will never *walk* out of here. But tell me, what is that prevents us from *flying?*

(Daedalus points skyward; he and Icarus laugh, and Icarus dashes offstage left, bringing back two sets of wings which he and Daedalus fit upon each other's shoulders as they kneel on ground.)

CHORUS MEMBER #2: Although the Labyrinth was enclosed by high walls, the top was not sealed.

CHORUS MEMBER #3: Daedalus designed wings for himself and his son.

CHORUS MEMBER #4: Instead of feathers, these wings were made of wax sealed with glue — light enough to catch the wind, yet strong enough to carry them far away from their prison on Crete.

ICARUS: You are truly a genius, father! With these wings we will sail through the sky like birds!

DAEDALUS: Icarus! We have no time for play. We must fly quickly to Sicily, where the King has offered us sanctuary. Stay behind me and do not fly close to the sun.

ICARUS: The sun! Home of the great god Apollo!

DAEDALUS: Icarus! It is time!

(Daedalus rises and begins to flap his wings, followed by Icarus; they walk slowly to left, where Poseidon appears, smiling with his trident raised.)

CHORUS MEMBER #1: Father and son rose from the Labyrinth at dawn, their wings catching a fresh sea breeze sent by Poseidon to aid them on the way.

(Daedalus, followed by Icarus, wends around the stage in a circle, moving from up left to up right and back to up left again.)

ICARUS: Look, father — there is Mount Olympus, home of the gods and goddesses!

(ATLAS, struggling to carry a large globe of the world upon his shoulders, enters from right and kneels at down right; PROMETHEUS, wrapped in chains, enters from left and kneels at down left.)

DAEDALUS: There is Atlas, who helped the Titans revolt against Zeus. He is condemned to bear the weight of the entire world upon his back from now until the end of time.
ICARUS: *(points at Prometheus)* And there, who is that wretched creature chained to a rock?
DAEDALUS: That is Prometheus, brother of Atlas. He offended the gods by giving fire to mankind. Zeus sent his servants, Force and Violence, to capture Prometheus and bind him so that birds may eat his flesh for all eternity.
ICARUS: Are the gods always so vengeful?
DAEDALUS: Only when they are afraid. For Fate, who is the most powerful deity of all, has decreed that Zeus will give birth to a son who will one day dethrone him and drive the gods from Olympus. Prometheus is the only one who knows who the mother of this boy will be.

(HERMES enters from right and glides across stage to Prometheus.)

ICARUS: Look, there is Hermes, messenger of Zeus!

DAEDALUS: At the start of each day, Zeus sends Hermes to ask Prometheus to tell the mother's name.

HERMES: Why suffer this endless torture, Prometheus? Let but one name pass your lips, and you will be free from Zeus' fury.

PROMETHEUS: I have committed no crime against Zeus. And nothing I say can free him from his fate.

(Hermes shrugs and exits left; Daedalus continues to circle the stage, but Icarus begins to lag behind, staring at the gods and goddesses who enter onstage; ARTEMIS, aiming a bow, enters from right and crosses to exit left; ARES, swinging a sword, enters from left and crosses to exit right.)

ICARUS: Father, there is Artemis, twin sister of Apollo! How winsome she is, and how strong! No wonder she is the protector of all wild things! And there is Ares, god of war! Bringer of strife and discord to the quarrels of mankind! A sullen fellow!

DAEDALUS: Icarus! Watch where you are going! Do not fly too high, or you will be ensnared by the rays of the sun!

ICARUS: *(laughs)* The sun of mighty Apollo? Apollo is a good god, father! He will not harm me! Look, there is Hephaestus, the blacksmith of the gods! And his wife, Aphrodite, goddess of beauty and love! Her voice is said to be the purest music in the universe!

DAEDALUS: Icarus, pay attention! You are drifting off course!

(Daedalus is at mid left, flapping furiously; Icarus is at down center, barely flapping his wings as AN EAGLE enters from right and approaches Icarus, who is entranced and begins following it around in a circle at center stage.)

EAGLE: Caw! Caw! Caw!

ICARUS: An eagle! This is the bird of Zeus! And it is calling me! Perhaps she will lead me to Mount Olympus and Zeus himself!

DAEDALUS: Icarus! Where are you going?

ICARUS: I am following the eagle, father!

DAEDALUS: No! Come back! You are flying too close to the sun!

EAGLE: Caw! Caw! Caw!

(Eagle flies offstage right; Icarus begins to stagger, as his wings droop.)

ICARUS: I, wait! Wait for me! I want to see Mount Olympus! I want to see the gods!

(Icarus swoons and staggers offstage left.)

ICARUS: My wings are melting! Help! I am falling! Falling!

DAEDALUS: Icarus! My son!

ICARUS: *(exits)* Aiieeeee!

(Daedalus hangs his head and kneels at mid left, wings over his head.)

CHORUS MEMBER #2: Icarus fell into the sea, and the waters of Poseidon closed above him.

CHORUS MEMBER #3: Though Daedalus, the most clever inventor of his age, was able to free his son from the Labyrinth—

CHORUS MEMBER #4: He could not free him from the reckless pursuit of his own dreams.

HESIOD: *(steps to down center)* And yet today, because of his bold folly, the flight of Icarus is one of our best-known myths. He is truly an immortal.

(LIGHTS OUT.)

THE END

Freya's Golden Necklace

Four of our days of the week are named for Norse gods: Tiu's Day (Tuesday), Woden's Day (Wednesday), Thor's Day (Thursday) and Freya's Day (Friday). The Norse tribes lived in Scandinavia and Germany from at least the first century B.C. and converted to Christianity by 1000 A.D. Their deities were warriors who fought monsters and tried to save the world from chaos. In many Norse myths, the gods have distinctly human personality traits and occasionally resort to disguise and subterfuge to achieve their ends. The 19th-century German composer Richard Wagner set many of these myths to music in a cycle of operas, one of which was called *Die Walküre*, or "The Valkyries," after the female spirits who determined the course of battles and conducted the dead warriors to their afterlife.

RUNNING TIME: 20 minutes

PLACE: Asgard, home of the Norse gods and goddesses

CAST: 12 actors, min. 4 boys (•), 4 girls (+)

- • Thor
- • Thrym
- + 3 Valkyries
- 4 Wedding Guests
- + Freya
- • Loki
- • Farmer

STAGE SET: 4' x 4' x 1' riser at mid center; flower stand at down left; table and stool at down right

PROPS: basket of apples; vase of flowers; the hammer

Miölnir shaped in the form of a three-foot-long thunder-bolt, made of cardboard or grey/black foam rubber

MUSIC: *Music for Valkyries*

COSTUMES: Thrym, Thor, Loki, Wedding Guests and Farmer wear Viking-style garb — robes, boots, fur vests, horned helmets with Thrym and Thor having more armor; Thor in disguise wears a face veil and a simple dress over his warrior costume; Valkyries wear black floor-length robes; Freya wears a green robe and a golden necklace, a garland of flowers in her hair

PRONUNCIATION:
Asgard — **As'**-gard
Freya — **Fray'**-a
Loki — **Lo'**-kee
Miölnir — **Myol'**-nir
Odin — **O'**-din
Valkyries — **Val'**-ke-rees

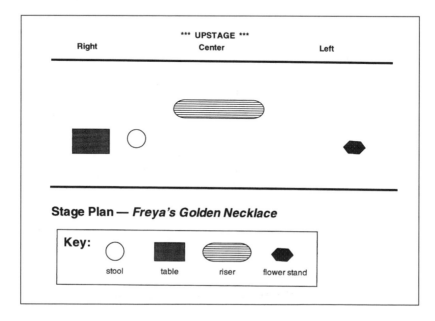

Stage Plan — *Freya's Golden Necklace*

Key: ◯ stool   ▬ table   ⬭ riser   ⬢ flower stand

(LIGHTS UP FULL on VALKYRIES standing on riser at mid center; they are singing as LOKI enters from right and crosses left; A FARMER enters from left, head bent down and carrying a basket of apples on his back as he crosses to right; Loki passes the farmer, turns and doubles back mischievously to catch him at down center.)

VALKYRIES: *(sing)* Welcome to Asgard, where the great gods and goddesses of Norseland feast and tell tales of bravery long into the cold winter night!

LOKI: *(to audience)* Why, if it isn't a farmer going to market with his harvest! *(taps Farmer on shoulder, points upward with great surprise)* By Odin's beard, is that a golden chariot in the sky?

(Farmer looks up, distracted, as Loki takes an apple from his basket and hides it behind his back.)

FARMER: Where, where?
LOKI: Right up there! By the flying monkey! Do you not see it?

(Farmer looks up again, and Loki takes a bite of the apple, hiding it when Farmer looks down.)

FARMER: Flying monkey! I see no monkey. Or a chariot. Aah! You must be a lunatic! *(trudges offstage right, mumbling)*
VALKYRIES: *(sing)* Loki…Loki…
LOKI: *(to audience)* No, my good friends, I am no lunatic — I am Loki! *(chuckles)* And I can be a very naughty, naughty little god.
VALKYRIES: *(sing)* Liar! Liar!
LOKI: All right, all right, I'm not an *actual* god. But I *know* a lot of gods! Odin, for instance, the boss of those loud-mouth Valkyries!

VALKYRIES: *(sing)* Odin! Odin!

LOKI: *(to Valkyries)* Give it a rest, will you! *(to audience)* Odin is the chief god of all Norseland, very wise, very brave. And Thor, I know Thor, the god of thunder and lightning, very strong, carries a big hammer, do *not* want to get on his bad side. And Heimdall, he's the watchman at the bridge leading into Asgard and Valhalla — that's Odin's fancy-schmancy palace. Heimdall has such powerful ears, he can hear the wool grow on the back of a sheep! *(chuckles)*

(FREYA enters from left and sets a vase of flowers on the stand at down left, then arranges them, humming.)

LOKI: Ah, but my favorite of them all is Freya, goddess of beauty and love! She rules over the bounty of nature and fills the world with good things for me to steal, er, borrow! Speaking of, um, uh, er borrowing...here's a myth you might enjoy — about Freya and her Golden Necklace. *(exits right)*

(THOR enters grumpily from left.)

VALKYRIES: *(sing)* Welcome, Thor, mighty Thor!

FREYA: Why, it is Thor! What a pleasant surprise! Come in to my palace!

THOR: Enter I shall, fair Freya. But it is a tale of woe I have come to tell.

FREYA: Tale of woe! What misfortune troubles mighty Thor?

THOR: My hammer, Miölnir, has been stolen.

VALKYRIES: *(sing)* Miölnir! The sacred hammer of Thor!

FREYA: The hammer you used to fashion the mountains and rivers of earth! The hammer that brings thunder to the skies and rain to the crops of mankind?

THOR: The same. Stolen by the giant Thrym and his giant cronies.

FREYA: How dare they!

THOR: When I find them, I will be sure to ask. But now, dear Freya, it is you whom I must ask for favor.

FREYA: Anything you wish! Anything that will deliver the scurrilous Thrym into the crushing grip of mighty Thor! Thor, proud defender of Asgard and slayer of serpents, trolls and dragons! Thor, the mightiest god in all creation! Tell me, Thor, what do you wish of me?

THOR: A dress.

VALKYRIES: *(sing)* A dress! A dress!

FREYA: I beg your pardon?

THOR: I need a dress.

VALKYRIES: *(sing)* A dress! Thor needs a dress!

THOR: *(to Valkyries)* Must you tell the whole world?

FREYA: Thor wishes a dress to fight the giant Thrym? This *is* a surprise!

THOR: I can explain…

(Loki enters from right wearing a dress and feathered boa and twirling an umbrella; he crosses to Thor and Freya.)

LOKI: Let me try. *(bows)*

FREYA: Loki! I might have known *you* were involved!

LOKI: But of course, your godliness! After I heard Thor's hammer was stolen, I took it upon myself to locate the culprits.

FREYA: Anticipating a fine reward, no doubt!

LOKI: My friendship with mighty Thor is the only reward I seek. But as I flew over the land of the giants, I saw Miölnir in the hands of Thrym and his giant friends.

THOR: My poor Miölnir!

LOKI: They were using it to play a game of "swat-the-cow-across-the-ocean."

VALKYRIES: *(sing)* Poor Miölnir!

FREYA: Surely Thrym knows he must return the hammer?

LOKI: He does, and he will — but for a price. Thrym said he would return Miölnir only if he could marry the goddess Freya.

FREYA: Me? Marry me?

VALKYRIES: *(sing)* Freya, marry Freya!

FREYA: Why, of all the nerve! To imagine that I — the goddess of beauty and love — could be coerced to give my hand to a thieving, ill-bred, half-witted, pin-headed, freak-faced ogre!

LOKI: I take it your answer is "no"?

FREYA: Valkyries!

VALKYRIES: *(sing)* No! Her answer is no!

THOR: Ahem…about the dress.

LOKI: You see, I, clever Loki, have devised a plan. You, dear goddess, must immediately send word to Thrym that you will marry him.

FREYA: What?

LOKI: Whereupon, Thor — disguised as you — will enter the giant's fortress. I will accompany Thor, disguised as your loyal handmaid. Together, we will reclaim the hammer of Thor!

THOR: Yes!

FREYA: That is the most ridiculous plan I have ever heard!

LOKI: Which is exactly why it will work. The bigger the giant, the smaller the brain.

THOR: Please, Freya, I am lonely for my Miölnir.

FREYA: Gods and their toys! All right, you may borrow one of my dresses, Thor. Please try to spill as little blood as possible.

THOR: Thank you, Freya!

LOKI: And we'll need that golden necklace, your godliness.

FREYA: My golden necklace?

VALKYRIES: *(sing)* Her golden necklace!

FREYA: This necklace was made for me at the beginning of time by the Zwerge, the dwarves who dwell in the dark hills above Asgard. I wear this necklace night and day, for if I were to lose it, all manner of evil would creep into the world.

LOKI: That is why Thor must have the necklace, or the giants will know he is an imposter.

THOR: I will be very careful, Freya. Upon my oath as the protector of Asgard!

FREYA: *(looks at Thor, then Loki, then Thor and sighs)* All right then.

(Freya takes off necklace and hands it to Thor; Loki reaches for necklace, Freya pulls it away.)

FREYA: Loki!

LOKI: *(backs away)* Sorry! Just force of habit. *(chuckles)*

(Thor exits left with necklace, followed by Freya; Loki strolls to down center.)

LOKI: Disguising Thor as Freya was a great plan. I thought it up myself. Of course, I had also given Thrym the idea of marrying Freya in the first place. I think they're all in for a big surprise! *(laughs)*

(Thor enters from left wearing a gown, a head garland, a veil and Freya's golden necklace; he is embarrassed and crosses to down center in small sideways steps.)

THOR: How do I look?

LOKI: Like something the werewolf dragged in. Remember, you've got to exude joy and happiness.

THOR: I will exude much joy and happiness when I get my hands on Thrym!

LOKI: Cheer up. It's your wedding day!

(THRYM and FOUR WEDDING GUESTS enter from

right; the Wedding Guests stand behind table and Thrym greets Loki leading/pulling a shy Thor by the hand.)

VALKYRIES: *(sing)* A wedding day in Giant Land! Guests gather for the feast! Thrym greets his blushing bride!

(Thrym bows and gestures for Thor to sit on stool; Thor sits, arms folded, legs crossed.)

THRYM: *(tries to lift Thor's veil)* Let me gaze upon her beauty!

LOKI: *(slaps Thrym's hand)* Now, now, my good giant. First things first. You promised the Goddess a special wedding gift, a gift befitting her godlike stature, er, status.

THRYM: And so I did! *(walks around Thor, inspecting him curiously)* Hmmm, stature...

LOKI: Is anything amiss, my lord?

THRYM: I never imagined Freya being so tall.

LOKI: She's just a dainty thing next to you, my lord.

THRYM: Doesn't say much, does she?

LOKI: My lord, she is struck dumb by your magnificence!

THRYM: *(tries to lift up veil but Thor turns away)* Let's have a look at those teeth!

LOKI: Leave her teeth alone! She is a goddess, not a horse! Where are your manners, sir giant?

THRYM: I am sorry. It's just that she looks so...so familiar.

LOKI: Familiar? Have you ever seen the goddess Freya before?

THRYM: No.

LOKI: Then how can she be familiar? *(shows golden necklace)* Here, see this necklace? It's made of purest gold.

WEDDING GUESTS: Aaahhh! Purest gold!

LOKI: It will be yours as part of her wedding dowry.

THOR: *(roars)* What? *(recover, repeats high-pitched)* What?

THRYM: Is something the matter with her throat?

LOKI: She swallowed an elf on the way up the mountain. May we see *your* wedding gift, O, giant?

THRYM: Of course. *(turns to Wedding Guests)* Bring in the wedding gift!

WEDDING GUEST #1: *(to Wedding Guest #2)* Bring in the wedding gift!

WEDDING GUEST #2: *(to Wedding Guest #3)* Bring in the wedding gift!

WEDDING GUEST #3: *(to Wedding Guest #4)* Bring in the wedding gift!

WEDDING GUEST #4: *(to curtain)* Bring in the — oh. Come on, you guys! It's a four-giant job!

(Wedding Guests exit right and re-enter dragging with difficulty a huge thunderbolt — Thor's hammer, Miölnir; Wedding Guest #4 drags the hammer and is dragged onstage by Wedding Guest #3, who is dragged on by Wedding Guest #2, who is dragged on by Wedding Guest #1; Wedding Guest #4 drops hammer in front of Thor.)

LOKI: The magic hammer of Thor! Wherever did you get it?

THRYM: From the foolish old goat himself! *(laughs)*

WEDDING GUEST #1: Thor never knew what hit him!

WEDDING GUEST #2: Like taking candy from a baby!

WEDDING GUEST #3: Some warrior-god!

WEDDING GUEST #4: If he's a warrior, I'm a pig knuckle!

(Thor begins to bristle; Loki calms him.)

LOKI: There, there — you wicked men have upset the goddess with your coarse humor. Why, everyone knows Thor has the strength of twenty — twenty mice, that is!

(Thrym and Wedding Guests laugh; Thor bristles, Loki shushes him.)

LOKI: Perhaps the goddess would care to examine her gift?

THRYM: *(slowly lifts hammer and gives handle to Thor)*

My, unngghh…unngghh, pleasure. There you are, my sweet. Isn't it splendid?

(Thor takes hammer, lifts it easily and smacks Thrym on top of head; Thrym swoons.)

THRYM: I think she loves me! *(falls, dies)*

(Wedding Guests charge Thor, who smacks them with hammer; they fall and die; in the fray, the golden necklace falls from Thor and is picked up by Loki, who hides it in his clothes.)

THOR: Miölnir! Good to see you, my friend!
VALKYRIES: *(sing)* Thor is avenged!
THOR: I am avenged! Come, Loki, let us return to Asgard!
LOKI: Asgard or bust!

(Thor trudges toward exit left, followed by a skipping Loki; just before reaching curtain, Thor stops.)

LOKI: What is it?
THOR: I feel like I am forgetting something.
LOKI: What?
THOR: I do not know. I have forgotten.
LOKI: You can't remember what you've forgotten? Or you've forgotten what you can't remember?
THOR: *(scratches his neck where the necklace should be)* I think I am just tired from killing a lot of giants. Let us not use our brains anymore for a while.
LOKI: Good idea. Lead on, mighty hammer-head!

(Thor exits; Loki pauses before curtain, holds up golden necklace.)

LOKI: He's probably looking for this. But that, my friends, is
    another myth for another time! *(laughs, exits)*
VALKYRIES: *(sing)* Loki! Naughty, naughty Loki! Loki! Loki!

(LIGHTS OUT.)

THE END

Music for Valkyries
(by L.E. McCullough)

© L.E. McCullough 1997

Music for Valkyries, pg. 2

Music for Valkyries, pg. 3

Gilgamesh and the Rose of Eternal Youth

This myth from ancient Sumeria presents the first mythic hero celebrated in world literature — Gilgamesh, King of Uruk, who leaves his kingdom to search for immortality. Gilgamesh was a real king of a city-state in the Sumerian Empire who lived sometime between 2700-2500 B.C. This epic tale of his adventures was written down on clay tablets around 2100 B.C. — over four thousand years ago! — and was the earliest such epic put down in writing. The story of the great flood that destroys the human race but for one man and his family, re-emerges in the Old Testament of the Bible as the story of Noah's Ark. It is found in some form in almost every mythology of every people in the world.

RUNNING TIME: 15 minutes

PLACE: Sumeria

CAST: 14 actors, min. 7 boys (•), 3 girls (+)

+ Siduri	• Gilgamesh, King of Uruk
3 Scorpion Men	• Urshanabi
• Utana-pishtim	• Enki
+ Ishtar	• Enlil
• Adad	+ Erish-kigal
• Shamash	Serpent

STAGE SET: rock at down right; rock at down left

PROPS: basket, 2 poles, small rose

EFFECTS: sound — thunder and lightning

COSTUMES: characters wear ancient Middle Eastern garb (robes and sandals) appropriate to their occupation and station, with the deities having more jewelry, head-dresses and finer robes; Scorpion Men should have grotesque scorpion masks and coverings; Serpent wears a snake mask and covering

PRONUNCIATION:
Adad — A-**dad**'
Enki — **En**'-kee
Enlil — En-**leel**'
Erish-kigal — Er-ish-**ki**'-gal
Gilgamesh — **Gil**'-ga-mesh
Ishtar — **Ish**'-tar
Shamash — Sha-**mash**'
Shurippak — **Shur**'-*i-pak*
Siduri — Si-**doo**'-*ree*
Urshanabi — Ursh-a-**na**'-bee
Uruk — **U**'-ruk
Utana-pishtim — U-**ta**'-na-**pish**'-tim

(LIGHTS UP FULL on SIDURI sitting on rock at down right, facing audience and rummaging through a basket at her feet; GILGAMESH enters from left, looking lost, then sees Siduri and approaches her.)

SIDURI: *(to audience)* My name is Siduri. I am a humble seller of fish from the great sea that borders the edge of the world. One day I saw a strange man dressed in crude animal skins wandering along the shore.

GILGAMESH: Fishwife!

SIDURI: He called out to me, and I was afraid because of the wild look in his eyes! *(shrinks away)*

GILGAMESH: Fishwife! I am Gilgamesh, King of strong-walled Uruk. What do you see that makes you fear me?

SIDURI: I see a man roaming the world trying to catch the wind.

GILGAMESH: Bah! Your words are nonsense! I have overthrown and killed Humbaba, who guarded the Cedar Forest. I have seized and slaughtered the Bull of Heaven. And I have slain the lions who guarded the mountain passes of Mitanni.

SIDURI: *(to audience)* The words he spoke were true. Gilgamesh was part man and part god, created by the Mother Goddess Nintu and given many gifts by the gods — great beauty by Shamash, great courage by Adad and great wisdom by Enki. But even as Gilgamesh ruled over the city-state of Uruk, he was not satisfied with his lot in life.

GILGAMESH: I wish to be *all* god! An immortal forever!

(Gilgamesh turns and heads toward up left; THREE SCORPION MEN enter from left and cross to mid center, blocking his way.)

SIDURI: And, thus, Gilgamesh set off on a great journey through the world. After many adventures, he came to

Mount Mashu and was surprised by three fierce Scorpion Men!

SCORPION MAN #1: What mortal dares tread this path?

GILGAMESH: I am Gilgamesh, King of strong-walled Uruk! Let me pass!

SCORPION MAN #2: Tell us the nature of your visit to this holy place!

GILGAMESH: I have come to find Utana-pishtim. I know he has found everlasting life and joined the assembly of the gods.

SCORPION MAN #3: No mortal has ever found Utana-pishtim. Go away at once!

GILGAMESH: I must see Utana-pishtim! Neither pain, nor sorrow, nor cold nor heat shall stop me!

SCORPION MAN #1: Very well. We shall open the gate.

SCORPION MAN #2: And you will pass into a tunnel that goes through the heart of the mountain.

SCORPION MAN #3: The tunnel is three hundred miles long — in complete darkness, every step!

GILGAMESH: Open the gate!

SCORPION MEN #1, 2 & 3: Open the gate!

(LIGHTS FADE TO BLACK; Scorpion Men exit left.)

SIDURI: And so Gilgamesh walked into the heart of the mountain, and he walked mile after mile after mile through the thick darkness. Fear flooded his soul, but he walked on. Finally, he came to the end of the tunnel. And to this shore, where I sit selling my fish.

(LIGHTS FADE UP FULL; Gilgamesh stands to left of Siduri, looking out at audience.)

GILGAMESH: I must cross to the other side of the sea!

SIDURI: Since the beginning of time, no human has traveled over these waters.

GILGAMESH: I must talk of life and death with Utana-pish-tim!

SIDURI: Then you must find Urshanabi the boatman to ferry you across.

(URSHANABI enters from left and stands at down center.)

URSHANABI. I am Urshanabi! Who summons me?

GILGAMESH: I am Gilgamesh and must cross the sea!

URSHANABI: It is a dangerous journey. First you must go into the forest and cut one hundred twenty poles, each one hundred feet long, and bring them to me.

SIDURI: And Gilgamesh went to the forest and brought back the poles.

(Gilgamesh picks up two poles on floor behind Siduri and carries them to Urshanabi; Gilgamesh and Urshanabi each take a pole and, facing left, mime poling a boat.)

URSHANABI: You must not let your hand touch the water, for these are waters of death that guard the land of the gods from intruders!

SIDURI: And for many days Gilgamesh and Urshanabi sailed across the waters of death to the land of the gods. On the other shore, Utana-pushtim awaited.

(UTANA-PISHTIM enters from left and sits on rock at down left, gazing across the stage.)

UTANA-PISHTIM: The boat of Urshanabi approaches. Who rides that is not her master?

(Gilgamesh steps forward to Utana-pushtim and bows; Urshanabi stands at down right.)

GILGAMESH: I am Gilgamesh, King of strong-walled Uruk. I seek Utana-pushtim.

UTANA-PISHTIM: I am he.

GILGAMESH: Then tell me the secret of everlasting life!

UTANA-PISHTIM: Does a bird build its nest to last forever? Does the river rise and flood its banks forever? Do brothers argue and dispute forever? Nothing is permanent in the world. The poorest beggar and richest king share the same fate — death. And is that not justly so?

GILGAMESH: But you were once mortal as I. How did you escape our common fate?

UTANA-PISHTIM: I will tell you a story. Many years ago, Enlil — ruler of all the gods — called his fellows together in council.

(ENLIL, ENKI, ISHTAR, ERISH-KIGAL, SHAMASH and ADAD enter from up right and stand at mid center in a semi-circle around Enlil.)

ENLIL: The people of the earth have become too many. They are noisy and dirty and destructive of the land we have given them. I want a great flood to come down upon them and wash these creatures away!

ISHTAR: I, Ishtar, goddess of love — and war — agree with Enlil. These humans disturb my sleep as well with their incessant clamor! What say you, Erish-kigal, my sister?

ERISH-KIGAL: I, Lord of the Underworld, am not as bothered by the human race as you gods who dwell above ground. But even so, my underworld is already nearly full of their dead!

ENLIL: What say you, Shamash, Lord of the Sun?

SHAMASH: It is time to clean up and start afresh!

ENLIL: What say you, Adad, Lord of Weather?

ADAD: Send down the rain!

ENLIL: And you, Enki, God of Wisdom?

ENKI: *(pauses)* I vote for. . . *(other gods stare at him, expectantly)* rain!

ENLIL, ISHTAR, ERISH-KIGAL, SHAMASH & ADAD: Rain! Rain! Rain!

(Enki leaves the semi-circle and crosses to Utana-pushtim.)

UTANA-PISHTIM: But in his heart, Enki did not fully agree with the other gods. He loved the imperfect humans and had given them much of his wisdom, teaching them how to grow crops and cultivate livestock. One night, Enki appeared to me in a dream.

ENKI: Utana-pushtim, King of Shurippak! Listen closely! The gods have decreed that a mighty flood will wash away the human race. You must build a giant ship and take aboard your family and the craftspeople of your town. Also, the seed of all living things — plants and birds and beasts.

UTANA-PISHTIM: I followed Enki's instructions. I built the giant ship and gathered my family. When the mighty rains began falling, we cast off from land into the open sea.

(LIGHTS FLICKER OFF AND ON; SOUND: THUNDER AND LIGHTNING.)

ENLIL: Hurricane, tornado and thunderstorm raged across the world!

ADAD: The land was shattered into pieces like a clay pot!

ERISH-KIGAL: The water buried the mountains and drowned every living thing!

UTANA-PISHTIM: Even the gods were humbled by the destruction!

(LIGHTS STOP FLICKERING; SOUND STOPS.)

ISHTAR: What terrible thing have we done?

SHAMASH: I, radiant Shamash, will spread my warmth upon the earth.

UTANA-PISHTIM: Our ship had come to rest on the slopes of Mount Nisir. Slowly the waters receded, and we found dry land. *(kneels)*

ADAD: *(points toward down left)* Look! Some humans have escaped the flood!

ENLIL: How can that be? Who permitted this?

ERISH-KIGAL: Enki is all-wise! Only he could have done this!

ENLIL: Enki, did you reveal the secret to the humans?

ENKI: I, my Lord Enlil? You do not give enough credit to your human creations. Utana-pushtim is a very wise human. He had a dream in which he discovered how to survive the flood.

ISHTAR: Then what are we to do with him and his family?

ENLIL: Utana-pushtim and his wife have preserved the seeds of earthly life. From this time forward, they will be immortal like the gods!

(LIGHTS FLICKER OFF AND ON; SOUND: THUNDER AND LIGHTNING; Enlil, Enki, Erish-kigal, Ishtar, Shamash and Adad exit up right; Urshanabi crosses to down center and faces right with his pole.)

GILGAMESH: I have searched the world for the secret of immortality. Yet, now I learn it is simply the whim of the gods!

UTANA-PISHTIM: Do not despair, Gilgamesh! The gods have given you many gifts. The gift of heroism. The gift of bravery. The gift of wisdom with which you rule your kingdom.

GILGAMESH: I will return to my people and share what I have learned on this journey.

(Gilgamesh crosses to down center and facing right, he and Urshanabi mime poling a boat.)

UTANA-PISHTIM: In appreciation of your long and dangerous voyage, I shall tell you of a heavenly secret. When you come near the shore, look down into the water. There you will see a rose growing at the bottom. The rose has many thorns, but if you can hold it, you will have the gift of eternal youth. You will not live forever, but you will be young and strong as long as you do live. *(exits left)*

(Gilgamesh stops poling and mimes reaching into water and pulling up a rose.)

GILGAMESH: I have it! The Rose of Eternal Youth!

(SERPENT enters from left, crawling along ground toward down center.)

SIDURI: But Gilgamesh was careless with the rose. As the boat reached shore, a serpent came out of the sea and stole the rose in its mouth!

(Serpent grabs rose from Gilgamesh and slithers off-stage left.)

GILGAMESH: The serpent has swallowed the rose!
URSHANABI: See how it sheds its skin and becomes younger!
GILGAMESH: Then I must finally accept my fate. When the gods created the world, they kept immortality for themselves and gave humans death. I shall never be a god!
SIDURI: But Gilgamesh did not despair. He returned to his kingdom to rule wisely and build many great monuments that have lasted through the centuries. For his journey had taught him a very important lesson — it is our deeds

that make us immortal. And if we wish to live in memory beyond our years, we can do so by making good use of our time in this life.

(LIGHTS OUT.)

THE END

King Midas and the Golden Touch

This myth was preserved for us by Ovid, a Latin poet who lived from 43 B.C. to 17 A.D. In his book of poems titled *Metamorphoses*, Ovid presented many tales from Greek and Roman mythology, including this one believed to have taken place in Phrygia, a kingdom located in the middle of what is now the nation of Turkey. Much of Roman mythology was drawn from Greek mythology, but Romans also believed that they were descended from the survivors of Troy, destroyed by the Greeks in the Trojan War. The myths surrounding the beginning of Rome are detailed in the *Aeneid*, an epic Latin poem by Virgil, written in the first century B.C.

RUNNING TIME: 20 minutes

PLACE: Phrygia

CAST: 14 actors, min. 3 boys (•), 6 girls (+)

- • Bacchus
- • King Midas
-   General
- + Temple Priestess
-   Physician
- + Calliope
- + Polyhymnia

- • Silenus
- + Chrysemeon, Midas' Daughter
-   Bursar
-   Admiral
- + Terpsichore
- + Thalia
-   Cook

STAGE SET: large chair at mid center with small table to the right

PROPS: bunch of grapes, accounting book, quill pen, wine cup, bowl with apple and orange, pointer

EFFECTS: sound — thunder and lightning; metallic clunk

COSTUMES: characters wear ancient Mediterranean dress appropriate to their occupation and station — togas and sandals, with jewelry and crowns for King Midas and Chrysemeon

PRONUNCIATION:
Bacchus -- **Bak'**-us
Calliope — Ka-**ly'**-o-pee
Chrysemeon— Kri-**se'**-mee-on
Mnemosyne — Mnee-mo-**sy'**-nee
Polyhymnia — Po-lee-**him'**-nee-a
Silenus — Si-**le'**-nus
Terpsichore — **Terp'**-si-kor
Thalia — **Thay'**-lee-a

(LIGHTS UP RIGHT on BACCHUS standing at down right, toying with a bunch of grapes.)

BACCHUS: *(to audience)*
    Hello. How do you do?
    I am Bacchus, god of revelry and wine.
    You do not recognize me? For shame!
    For we have met together many a time!

    With my fermented fruit, I bring joy to your nights
    Though your head may ache sore in the morning.
    Too many sips, and over you tip—
    Good judgment flees without warning!

    Men round the world pay homage to me,
    Craving the juice from the vine;
    Believing themselves mighty and bold,
    While they stumble, feeble and blind.

    Let me tell you the story of a King
    Who lived in Phrygia long centuries ago.
    Midas was his name, and oft-sad he was
    For of money he always ran low. *(exits right)*

(LIGHTS UP CENTER AND LEFT; KING MIDAS sits on large chair at mid center, his BURSAR standing at his right holding a quill pen and an open accounting book.)

KING MIDAS:
    No, it cannot be!
    It cannot be at all!
    The treasury is nearly empty again,
    And more creditors come to call?

BURSAR:
    My King, you are a glorious king
    Who has won many a war and battle.
    But the way this kingdom runs through gold
    It's like feeding turnips to cattle!

(GENERAL enters from left, stands at left of King Midas, bows.)

KING MIDAS:
Ah, dear General, leader of my troops!
What news from the Persian front?

GENERAL:
The news is grave, fair monarch,
Forgive me if I sound blunt—

But the soldiers, brave fighters to the last,
Have not been paid in almost a year.
And if I return without their due,
A mutiny is certain, I fear!

BURSAR:
Munity!

KING MIDAS: *(stands)*
Not mutiny!

GENERAL:
Mutiny and worse, I predict!

KING MIDAS:
Then, Bursar, go and write him a check
And write it double-quick! *(sits)*

(General takes check from Bursar and exits right; ADMIRAL enters from left, stands at left of King Midas, bows.)

ADMIRAL:
As Admiral of the navy,
I deliver this somber report.
All of our warships are rusting
And springing up leaks by the quart!

BURSAR:
>   And if we do not repair them,
>   Will they sink to the ocean floor?

KING MIDAS:
>   Then that is a fitting solution
>   To this expensive nautical chore!

(King Midas waves Admiral off and turns away; Admiral takes check from Bursar and exits right; TEMPLE PRIESTESS enters from left, stands at left of King Midas, bows.)

KING MIDAS:
>   Ah, here comes the Temple Priestess
>   To announce an upcoming feast!
>   Or welcome perhaps a new deity
>   Arrived recently from the East!

TEMPLE PRIESTESS:
>   Indeed, dear Sire, I bring good news;
>   Another goddess has joined our shrine!
>   And the statue we erect in her honor
>   Will cost only a million or nine!

KING MIDAS: *(stands)*
>   Haven't we enough divinities
>   To last to the end of all time?
>   The way your temple spends money,
>   You'd think frugality was a crime!

(Bursar starts to write a check but hesitates and looks at King Midas.)

KING MIDAS: Oh, go on! Write her a check for the silly statue! *(sits)*

(Temple Priestess takes check from Bursar and exits right; PHYSICIAN enters from left, stands at left of King Midas, bows.)

BURSAR:
Announcing the royal Physician
On business of urgent degree!

KING MIDAS:
Urgent I'm sure to his wallet!
What else can it possibly be?

PHYSICIAN:
King Midas, I come not for my sake;
It's your daughter, young Chrysemeon.
She has a mysterious malady
That renders her sickly and wan.

KING MIDAS: *(stands)*
What? My daughter lies ailing?
She must be healed without delay!
(grabs Bursar and shoves him toward Physician)
Buy all the medicine in Phrygia—
Then to her bedside be quickly away!

(Bursar hurriedly writes a check to Physician, who grabs it and rushes offstage right.)

KING MIDAS: Away!

(Bursar rushes offstage right; King Midas crosses to down center.)

KING MIDAS:
Oh, what I'd give for more money!
An endless supply of pure wealth!

This kingdom is costing me dearly
And ruining my composure and health!

*(SILENUS enters from left, holding a wine cup; swaying
and hiccupping, he crosses to down center and stops in
front of King Midas as if he had just seen him that
instant.)*

SILENUS:
Oh! There you are, my good fellow!
I knew you were lurking someplace!
Say, have you seen a chap name of Midas?
I've a message to give him post haste.

KING MIDAS:
I am that chap name of Midas,
Commonly referred to as "King"!
Just whom shall I say is asking,
Before your neck is put in a sling?

SILENUS: *(shakes King Midas' hand vigorously)*
My name is Silenus of Delphi—
Brother to the mighty god Pan,
Whose flute rings through the forest
In each and every land.

Returning from a symposium,
I somehow fell astray;
And now I express my gratitude
For taking me in your palace this way!

KING MIDAS: *(draws his hand away)* I did?

SILENUS:
You have been the very soul of hospitality and friendship! *(shakes King Midas' hand vigorously)*

KING MIDAS: *(draws his hand away)* I have?

SILENUS: And I would like to repay you! *(shakes King Midas' hand vigorously; this time King Midas does not draw away)*

KING MIDAS: You would?

SILENUS:
Of course! But I...er, that is to say, *me*—
Which is the same mostly as *I*—
Have no actual wealth of my own—
Which is to say, *my* pockets are dry!

KING MIDAS: Bah! *(draws away from Silenus)*

SILENUS:
But if your kingship will consent
With me a small journey to take,
My master is prepared to reward you
And grant any wish you should make!

KING MIDAS: And who *is* your master, old man?

SILENUS:
Why, Bacchus, dispeller of boredom—
The rollicking god of good cheer!
And, if my ears aren't deceiving,
I believe it is him who draws near!

(BACCHUS enters from right and crosses to down center standing to right of King Midas, with Silenus on King Midas' left; Bacchus offers a grape to King Midas, who accepts it.)

BACCHUS:
> How pleasant to be among mortals!
> The merriest creatures under the sky!
> Tell, O Midas, what you wish of me—
> Twill be yours in a twinkling of an eye!

KING MIDAS: I wish for great wealth — as much as I can touch!

BACCHUS: *(laughs loudly)* Ha-ha-ha-ha!

KING MIDAS: You find that amusing?

BACCHUS: Oh, yes — very much!

> With a universe full of marvels
> And wondrous mysteries manifold,
> The gods can only laugh
> When men pray to them for gold!

> But no matter, I am quite generous,
> And your wish is hereby made.
> So now I give the greatest wealth
> A mortal being can surely crave!

> *(points to stage left)* Muses, come forth!

(TERPSICHORE, CALLIOPE, POLYHYMNIA and THALIA dance out from left to down center and address King Midas.)

CALLIOPE, POLYHYMNIA, THALIA & TERPSICHORE:
> We are fair sister Muses,
> Daughters of Zeus and Mnemosyne;
> With inspiration to the mind
> We guide creations large and tiny.

CALLIOPE:
　　I am Calliope,
　　Muse of poetry most profound;
　　With metaphor and meter,
　　I make your verse resound.

POLYHYMNIA:
　　I am Polyhymnia,
　　Muse of melody divine;
　　My airs and gentle harmonies
　　Will soothe your troubled mind.

THALIA:
　　I am the Muse of comedy,
　　And Thalia is my name;
　　With my wit and jollity,
　　I help playwrights win acclaim.

TERPSICHORE:
　　And I am flowing Terpsichore,
　　Muse of rhythm and of dance;
　　Your worries will fast depart, my King,
　　When together we do prance.

KING MIDAS: *(to Bacchus)*
　　Is this some sort of lunacy?
　　Some perverse, peculiar prank?
　　I asked for wealth and riches —
　　Not a bunch of arty cranks!

SILENUS: *(to King Midas)*
　　The scholars and sages do tell us
　　That the Muses and their guests
　　Are the greatest of the godly gifts
　　Any human can possess.

BACCHUS:
>But Midas I see is unsatisfied
>With splendid powers of the mind;
>His only desire is riches
>Of the sordid, common kind.
>
>Thus I shall grant his treaty
>To have abundant wealth untold;
>And give to him the magic touch
>That turns everything to gold.

KING MIDAS: Yes!

(Bacchus extends his right arm and points at King Midas; LIGHTS FLICKER QUICKLY ON AND OFF; SOUND: THUNDER AND LIGHTNING OFFSTAGE; King Midas staggers and whirls as Four Muses exit left followed by Silenus and Bacchus.)

KING MIDAS: *(rights himself at down center)*
>By the silver beard of Jupiter
>That was a most frenetic dream!
>Or was it, upon reflection,
>Quite the fantasy it seems?

(King Midas holds up grape and examines it with awe.)

KING MIDAS:
>By Juno, I don't believe it!
>It makes my blood run chilling cold!
>This grape I took from Bacchus
>Has turned to purest gold!

(Bursar enters from right carrying quill and accounting book.)

KING MIDAS:
O, Bursar!
Bring to me your quill!

BURSAR:
Certainly, my King.
Have you a task for me to fill?

(Bursar holds out quill; King Midas takes it and a smile spreads over his face.)

KING MIDAS:
By the hammer of Vulcan
The quill has turned to gold!

BURSAR:
It must be some illusion,
If I may make so bold!

KING MIDAS: *(grabs accounting book)*
Here! See how the pages of this tome
Turn bright yellow at my touch!

BURSAR:
This is truly an enchantment—
Some wizard spell or such!

(King Midas crosses to mid center and puts quill and book on table; he lays his hands on table and stares in wonder.)

KING MIDAS:
Gold! Gold! Gold!
A table of gold — bright as the sun!
(touches chair with his thumb)
And now the chair turns to metal
With but the slightest touch of my thumb!

BURSAR:
How strange the Fates that rule us!
How odd the gifts they send!
Why, your lack of funds this morning
Had you very near wits' end!

KING MIDAS:
And now I can mint a treasury
With a golden wave of my hand!
I will be the richest King
To rule o'er any land!

(General enters from right and stands at down right.)

KING MIDAS:
If I need an army,
Or two or three or ten,
I can buy a dozen regiments,
Each with half a million men!

(Admiral enters from right and stands next to General.)

BURSAR:
And what about the navy?

KING MIDAS:
I'll buy warships by the pound!

BURSAR:
And when they spring a leak?

KING MIDAS:
I'll just have them melted down!

(Temple Priestess enters from right and stands next to General and Admiral.)

KING MIDAS:
>Statues for the temple?
>Build as many as you can pile!
>Our gods will be the envy
>From Nineveh to the Nile!
>
>And now to celebrate our fortune,
>Let us have a gala feast!

BURSAR:
>And honor wise King Midas—
>May his golden touch never cease!

(King Midas sits at table as Bursar, General, Admiral and Temple Priestess gather behind; COOK enters from left and sets a wine cup and a bowl containing an apple and orange in front of King Midas.)

KING MIDAS: *(picks up apple)*
>Ah, a red delicious apple,
>So round and ripe and firm!

(King Midas bites into apple and yelps in pain; SOUND: METALLIC CLUNK OFFSTAGE.)

KING MIDAS: *(holds apple in air)*
>By the bow of fair Diana,
>Did I bite into a worm?

COOK: *(gasps)*
>Sire, the apple is no longer red!
>It is yellow and glitters bright!

(King Midas drops apple on table, pauses and grabs orange, bites into it and yelps in pain. SOUND: METALLIC CLUNK OFFSTAGE.)

KING MIDAS: *(holds orange in air)*
    This orange, it is rotten!
    Hard as an iron nail!
    How dare you serve your King this way—
    I'll have you thrown in jail!

COOK:
    Nay, Sire, when laid upon the table,
    The food was fresh as ever before;
    But after meeting your grasping fingers,
    It became a lump of ore!

(King Midas stands and grabs the wine cup; he raises it slowly in the air, tilts his head back and tries to drink; SOUND: METALLIC CLUNK OFFSTAGE; King Midas throws down the cup.)

BURSAR, GENERAL, ADMIRAL, TEMPLE PRIESTESS
& COOK:
    The wine has turned to stone!
    The King's wine has turned to stone!

(Bursar, General, Admiral, Temple Priestess and Cook gasp and recoil from King Midas who grips table intensely.)

KING MIDAS: Send for the Physician at once!

(Cook exits right; Physician enters from right carrying a pointer, which he uses to poke apple and orange.)

PHYSICIAN:
    This is indeed a wizard spell!
    A wonder to behold!
    Everything the King does touch
    Turns instantly to gold!

(King Midas' daughter, CHRYSEMEON, enters from left and crosses slowly to mid center.)

BURSAR, GENERAL, ADMIRAL & TEMPLE PRIESTESS:
Chrysemeon, daughter of the king! *(bow)*

CHRYSEMEON:
Oh, father, I have heard the news,
And am filled with sadness so!
What can I do to offer aid
In this time of trial and woe?

KING MIDAS:
Alas, my dearest Chrysemeon,
I stand ashamed before your eyes.
You see how the lust for riches
Has led to my demise.

CHRYSEMEON:
I cannot stand to view you thus,
Unable to drink or eat!
Oh, father, let me comfort you
In your hour of defeat!

(Chrysemeon runs up and embraces King Midas, who tries to pull away but cannot before she touches him; as soon as she touches him, she turns into a gold statue and freezes in place.)

KING MIDAS: No! *(backs away from Chrysemeon)*
BURSAR: She is frozen into a statue,
GENERAL: A shiny marvel to behold.
ADMIRAL: I wonder will this finally quench
TEMPLE PRIESTESS: Her father's thirst for gold?

(Bursar, General, Admiral, Temple Priestess and Physician circle one time around Chrysemeon and exit right.)

KING MIDAS:
No, by the gods and goddesses,
This tragedy cannot be!
My only child Chrysemeon—
Made silent forever...by me!

(King Midas falls to knees and hangs head; Bacchus enters from left, holding grapes.)

BACCHUS:
All conquering are these heady grapes
Made from the heavenly vine.
They make the weak and craven feel
Like gods in their own mind.

So beware, you foolish mortals
Who invoke the deities in jest.
For your wish just might be granted
And — well, you know the rest!

(LIGHTS OUT.)

THE END

The Monkey King

The founder of Buddhism was Siddhartha Gautama (563-483 B.C.), an Indian nobleman who at age 29 renounced the pleasures of the world and began a search for a solution to the problems of death and human suffering. After achieving a spiritual enlightenment (the word "Buddha" is Sanskrit for "the Enlightened One"), Gautama spent the rest of his life traveling and teaching his doctrines. Like the other major religion of India, Hinduism, Buddhism posits a belief in *reincarnation*, or the return of the human spirit over many lifetimes in many forms that may include animals as well as people. Through the centuries, the stories told of the Buddha's numerous lives were gathered into a collection known as The Jataka Tales. The song that accompanies this play, *The Monkey King*, can be heard on the CD *Songs of the Jataka Tales* by singer/songwriter Penny Nichols of Saugerties, New York (KTD Dharma Goods, 616/796-2944).

RUNNING TIME: 15 minutes

PLACE: India

CAST: 14 actors, min. 3 boys (•), 2 girls (+) and Offstage Vocal Chorus

+ Grandmother	• Boy
+ Girl	• Monkey King
6 Monkeys	• Brahmadatta, King of Benares
Fisherman	2 Servants

STAGE SET: small riser at down right; scrim of mango tree and large rock at mid center; throne (chair) at down left

PROPS: book, mango (green rubber ball), fisherman's net, tree branches (palms), stick (3 feet in length)

MUSIC: *The Monkey King* by Penny Nichols (© 1994 Karma Kagyu Institute, Choyang Music/BMI)

COSTUMES: Grandmother, Boy and Girl wear modern casual dress; Brahmadatta, Servants and Fisherman wear ancient Indian garb appropriate to their occupation and station, a headdress and shiny robe for Brahmadatta, shields for Servants; Monkeys wear masks and body coverings

PRONUNCIATION:
    Benares — Be-**na'**-rez
    Brahmadatta — Bra-ma-**da'**-ta
    Ganges — **Gan'**-geez
    Himalaya — Hi-ma-**lay'**-a
    Jataka — **Ja'**-ta-ka

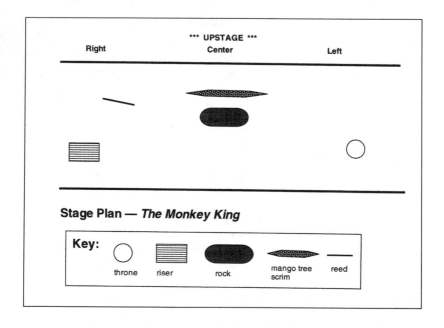

Stage Plan — *The Monkey King*

Key: throne, riser, rock, mango tree scrim, reed

(LIGHTS UP RIGHT on GRANDMOTHER sitting in lotus-position on small riser at down right, reading a book; GIRL and BOY enter from right, arguing, and stop at left of Grandmother.)

GIRL: You don't know what you're talking about!

BOY: I do so!

GIRL: Do not!

BOY: Do so!

GIRL: Not!

BOY: Do!

GIRL: I'm going to ask Grandmother!

BOY: I'm asking first!

GRANDMOTHER: Someone has a question?

GIRL: *(pause)* You ask!

BOY: No, you!

GIRL: *(clears throat)* Grandmother, he says a person can become perfect. Any person at all.

BOY: Absolutely, totally and completely perfect!

GIRL: But that's impossible!

BOY: And without homework or braces!

GRANDMOTHER: Who told you this?

BOY: We're studying world history in school, and we read about the Buddha in ancient India. Our teacher said the Buddha was a man who learned how to achieve perfection.

GIRL: But the Buddha lived twenty-five hundred years ago! If he had the secret of perfection, how come there aren't any perfect people around today?

GRANDMOTHER: Your teacher was right — the Buddha *did* outline a path for human beings to achieve perfection.

BOY: Told you!

GIRL: *(sticks out tongue)* I knew it already!

GRANDMOTHER: But it's not that simple. The Buddha taught that true perfection can only be achieved by living a great many lives and by learning a new lesson in each life.

GIRL: How come you can't get perfect in one life? Isn't that the most perfect way?

GRANDMOTHER: The kind of perfection the Buddha spoke of isn't about *getting*. It's about *giving*.

BOY: I don't understand.

GRANDMOTHER: Sit down and I'll tell you a story. *(Girl and Boy sit next to Grandmother.)* This book is a book of Jataka Tales, or stories of the different lives lived by the Buddha. Most often he came to earth as an animal — a deer, a rabbit, maybe a swan or an elephant. Once upon a time, he appeared as a great king of monkeys.

(LIGHTS UP CENTER; on rock at mid center MONKEY KING sits serenely, surrounded by SIX MONKEYS who frolic and mime eating mangos.)

GRANDMOTHER: High in the Himalaya Mountains, underneath the shade of a beautiful mango tree, dwelt a Monkey King and his tribe of eighty thousand monkeys. The monkeys were very happy and lived in peace and harmony, eating the delicious mango fruit. But they were also very careful.

MONKEY KING: The Ganges River, the mightiest river in all India, flows past our beloved tree to the valley below. And so we must beware — do not let even the smallest blossom fall into the water!

MONKEY #1: Or the river will carry it through the mountains!

MONKEY #2: And into the city!

MONKEY #3: Where the beautiful fruit might be found by *men*!

MONKEY #4: Who, filled with desire for its goodness, would search for the tree!

MONKEY #5: Following the river into the mountains!

MONKEY #6: Until they discovered our kingdom!

MONKEY KING: And we would have to flee!

(OFFSTAGE VOCAL CHORUS SINGS. MUSIC: "The Monkey King." While Monkey King sits serenely, Monkeys frolic around rock, tossing one mango among them. LIGHTS UP LEFT; BRAHMADATTA sits on throne at down left, attended by TWO SERVANTS standing on either side.)

CHORUS: *(sings)*
Once the king of Monkeys lived in a mango tree,
With eighty thousand of his very best friends,
They lived happy and free.
One ripe mango fell into the river
And floated down a ways.
The King of Benares was bathing that day,
When the mango came, they heard him say:

"What a beautiful mango, divine mango,
I could eat mangos all day.
What a beautiful mango, divine mango,
I could eat mangos all day."

(A FISHERMAN enters from right and stands at down center, casting with his net; a mango rolls away from the Monkeys to down center where it is netted by Fisherman.)

GRANDMOTHER: Despite the precautions taken by the monkeys, one day a mango fell from the tree into the river. It floated downstream to the city below, and lodged in the net of a fisherman.

FISHERMAN: *(picks up mango)* What is this wondrous fruit? I must show it to King Brahmadatta!

(Fisherman rushes to throne and hands mango to Servant #1, who hands it to Servant #2, who bows and presents it to Brahmadatta.)

BRAHMADATTA: This is a most exceptional fruit! I have never seen its like!

SERVANT #1: It is a mango, my king.

BRAHMADATTA: A mango! Where on earth grows such a thing?

SERVANT #2: Not in our valley, sire, but in the mountains above.

BRAHMADATTA: Then, we must go to the mountains at once, and find the tree that bore this fruit!

(OFFSTAGE VOCAL CHORUS SINGS. MUSIC: "The Monkey King." Two Servants help Brahmadatta to stand, and they advance in slow march to mid center, followed by Fisherman. Monkey King remains seated on top of rock; Monkeys peer out from behind rock, one or two holding up palms that shield Monkey King from view of humans.)

CHORUS: *(sings)*
"Find the tree that made this fruit,"
Said the king to his gathered men;
Way up the river in the Himalayas,
That's where the mangos have been.
So they sailed upstream till they saw the tree,
And ate the mangos till they fell asleep.
But during the night the king woke up,
To find eighty thousand monkeys in his mango tree!

They were eating mangos, beautiful mangos,
Mangos all night long.
They were eating mangos, beautiful mangos,
Mangos all night long.

SERVANT #1: We have reached the mango tree, my king.

BRAHMADATTA: It is as beautiful as I imagined! But what are those shadows moving on the branches?

SERVANT #2: Monkeys, sire. Many thousands of monkeys.

BRAHMADATTA: Monkeys! On *my* mango tree? Surround the tree and prevent their escape. At dawn we will shoot them! And eat them for supper with fresh mangos!

(Brahmadatta, Two Servants and Fisherman kneel on ground, heads lowered as if asleep; Monkeys rise and circle Monkey King.)

MONKEY #1: These savages have come to steal our mangos!

MONKEY #2: And then kill us!

MONKEY #3: And then eat us!

MONKEY #4: They surround our tree!

MONKEY #5: Escape is impossible!

MONKEY #6: What are we to do, dear master?

MONKEY KING: Fear not, little ones. Fear not, but do as I say.

(Monkey King jumps down from rock and hops to mid right, where he picks up stick and carefully lays it down on ground pointing to up right as Monkeys cluster around rock watching him.)

MONKEY #1: Look at him fly through the air!

MONKEY #2: The Monkey King has jumped to a tree on the river bank!

MONKEY #3: He has taken a very long bamboo reed from the edge of the water!

MONKEY #4: He will tie the reed between the two trees!

MONKEY #5: Making a bridge to escape!

MONKEY #6: And we will not be eaten!

(Monkey King lies down on ground, head pointed up

right, arms outstretched and holding the end of the stick as if he is suspended in mid-air.)

MONKEY #1: But wait! The reed is too short!
MONKEY #2: He has tied the end of the reed to his paw!
MONKEY #3: The Monkey King clings to the branch!
MONKEY #4: He is part of the bridge!

(Brahmadatta, Two Servants and Fisherman awake and rise.)

MONKEY #5: He wants us to run over his back to freedom!
MONKEY #6: Look out! Here come the archers!

(Monkeys run "over" [alongside] Monkey King and exit up right as Two Servants mime shooting arrows and Fisherman waves his net. OFFSTAGE VOCAL CHORUS SINGS. MUSIC: "The Monkey King.")

CHORUS: *(sings)*
All of the monkeys crossed the river,
Walking on the back of their king.
He risked his life for the sake of his people,
He has won everything.

(Monkey #6 is the last to cross; he is scared to jump and Two Servants aim their bows at him.)

MONKEY KING: Come on, you can do it!
SERVANT #1: I've got my eye on this one!
MONKEY KING: Jump! Now!
SERVANT #2: This monkey is mine!
MONKEY #6: Aaaaiii!

(Monkey #6 jumps and lands hard on the Monkey King's back.)

MONKEY KING: Aaauugh!

FISHERMAN: The big monkey's back is broken!

MONKEY #6: My king!

MONKEY KING: Never mind me! Save yourself! Run!

(Monkey #6 skitters offstage up right as the injured Monkey King rolls over and is seized by the Two Servants and Fisherman.)

BRAHMADATTA: Bring him to me!

(Brahmadatta steps to down center and Monkey King is brought to him, held up between the Two Servants.)

FISHERMAN: Shall we cook him for supper, my king?

BRAHMADATTA: Cook him? You shall bathe him in sweet perfumes and give him sweet water to drink! This brave creature has shown more courage than a hundred of my generals!

(Brahmadatta kneels before Monkey King.)

BRAHMADATTA: You made of your body a bridge for others. Did you not know your own life would be lost? Who are you, Blessed One, and who are these monkeys?

MONKEY KING: O Brahmadatta, I am their chief and their guide. I was their father and I loved them. I do not suffer in dying, because I have won their freedom.

BRAHMADATTA: Your death is a great lesson to me!

MONKEY KING: Then I die twice happy. Remember it is not your sword that makes you king. It is the love you have for your people. Rule not through power because they are your subjects. Rule through love because they are your children. *(dies)*

GRANDMOTHER: And the Monkey King died. A temple was

built for him in Benares, and the Brahmadatta ruled his people with love for many years.

(Two Servants and Fisherman solemnly take Monkey King offstage left, followed by Brahmadatta. OFFSTAGE VOCAL CHORUS SINGS. MUSIC: "The Monkey King.")

CHORUS: *(sings)*
    The Monkey King was a mighty king,
    The King of Benares saw.
    As he watched them go across the river,
    Happy and free after all.

    It's all for the mangos, beautiful mangos,
    All for the sake of these mango trees.
    It's all for the mangos, beautiful mangos,
    All for the sake of these trees.
    All for the sake of these trees.
    All for the sake of these trees.

(LIGHTS OUT.)

THE END

The Monkey King
(words & music by Penny Nichols, arr. by L.E. McCullough)

♩ = 130

Once the king of Mon- keys lived in a man- go

tree, with eigh- ty thou- sand of his ve- ry best friends,

they lived hap- py and free. One ripe man- go fell

in- to the ri- ver and float- ed down a ways. The

King of Be- na- res was bath- ing that day, when the

man- go came, they heard him say: "What a beau- ti- ful man- go,

The Monkey King, pg. 2

di- vine man- go, I could eat man- gos all day. What a

beau- ti- ful man- go, di- vine man- go, I could eat man- gos all

day." "Find the tree that made this fruit," said the

king to his gath- ered men; Way up the ri- ver in the

Hi- ma- lay- as, that's where the man- gos have been. So they

sailed up- stream till they saw the tree, and ate the man- gos till they

The Monkey King, pg. 3

fell a- sleep. But dur- ing the night the king woke up, to find

eigh- ty thous-and mon-keys in his man- go tree! They were eat- ing man-gos,

beau- ti- ful man- gos, man- gos all night long. They were

eat- ing man- gos, beau- ti- ful man- gos, man- gos all night

long. All of the mon- keys crossed the ri- ver,

walk- ing on the back of their king. He risked his life for the

The Monkey King, pg. 4

sake of his peo- ple, he has won eve- ry- thing.

The Mon- key King was a migh- ty king, the

King of Be- na- res saw. As he watched them go a-

cross the ri- ver, hap- py and free af- ter all. It's

all for the man- gos, beau- ti- ful man- gos, all for the sake of

man- go trees. It's all for the man- gos, beau- ti- ful man- gos,

all for the sake of these trees. All for the sake of these

trees. All for the sake of these trees.

How Quetzalcoatl Found the Sun

Since at least 1500 B.C., Mexico and the rest of Mesoamerica have been home to many civilizations — the Olmecs, Zapotecs, Toltecs, Aztecs and Mayans — which shared many mythological figures among them. Some of the region's gods and goddesses are represented as being part animal, such as the jaguar, crocodile and various birds. The god Quetzalcoatl was believed to be half god-half serpent; he was a benevolent god who taught humans about agriculture, industry and the arts while fighting against his evil sibling gods, the Tezcatlipocas, who constantly tried to destroy the world. Even so, the ancient Mesoamericans believed the universe will end by earthquakes at the close of El Quinto Sol — the Fifth Sun — a period in which we are now living.

RUNNING TIME: 20 minutes

PLACE: Mexico

CAST: 14 actors, min. 2 boys (•), 3 girls (+)

+ Grandmother	+ Granddaughter
• Ometeotl	+ Omecihuatl
Red Tezcatlipoca	Blue Tezcatlipoca
Black Tezcatlipoca	• Quetzalcoatl
Lizard	Jaguar
Monkey	Woodpecker
Rabbit	Eagle

STAGE SET: small riser at down right; large rock at mid center

PROPS: *metate* (3-legged stone grinding table), roller, tortilla, 2 sticks, hand mirror

EFFECTS: Sound — woodpecker beak striking rock

MUSIC: *A La Víbora* (a favorite children's game in Mexico)

COSTUMES: Grandmother and Granddaughter wear modern Mexican folk dress; Animals wear appropriate masks and coverings; divine characters wear Aztec garb — Red Tezcatlipoca wears red robe and headdress, etc.; Quetzalcoatl wears a long feathered head plume, rainbow-colored robe and gold jewelry and a cloak

PRONUNCIATION:
    Ometeotl — O-me-te-**o'**-tl
    Omecihuatl — O-me-cee-**wha'**-tl
    Quetzalcoatl — Ketz-al-**ko'**-tl
    Tezcatlipoca — Tez-cat-lee-**po'**-ca

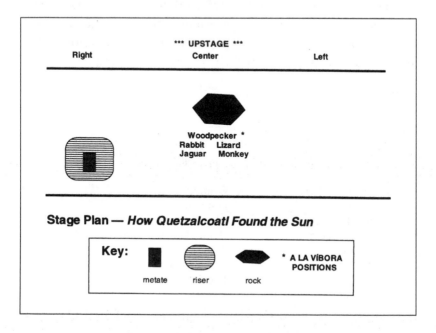

Stage Plan — *How Quetzalcoatl Found the Sun*

(LIGHTS UP RIGHT on GRANDMOTHER sitting at down right on a small riser, rolling a tortilla on a metate; GRANDDAUGHTER enters from right and sits next to her.)

GRANDDAUGHTER: Grandmother, I am so excited! The fiesta is going to start tonight! Do you need help making tortillas?

GRANDMOTHER: No, but you may set the table for supper. That is the task my grandmother gave me when I was your age.

GRANDDAUGHTER: *My* age? Did they have fiestas in Mexico that long ago?

GRANDMOTHER: Ha! You are such a joker, mi nieta! People have celebrated fiesta for many centuries, almost before time itself.

GRANDDAUGHTER: And have they always had tortillas?

GRANDMOTHER: They had no tortillas until they had corn. And to have corn, the people needed the sun.

GRANDDAUGHTER: But wasn't the sun always in the sky?

GRANDMOTHER: Ha! You joke with me again! Surely you have heard the story of how Quetzalcoatl found the sun?

(Granddaughter shakes head "no.")

GRANDMOTHER: Then listen closely, so that you may tell *your* grandchildren what I tell *you* now.

(LIGHTS UP LEFT AND CENTER as OMETEOTL and OMECIHUATL enter from left, each carrying sticks; they stop at down center and face audience, sticks held in front of them.)

GRANDMOTHER: Many thousands and hundreds of thousands of years ago, here in the land of Mexico, the universe was created by a god, Ometeotl, and his wife, the goddess Omecihuatl.

(Ometeotl, and his wife, Omecihuatl point and shake sticks at audience; LIZARD, JAGUAR, MONKEY, WOODPECKER, RABBIT and EAGLE enter from left and dance to rock at mid center, where they sit)

GRANDMOTHER: They created the creatures of our world — the lizard and jaguar, monkeys, woodpeckers, rabbits and eagles. They also created their own four divine children, the four Tezcatlipocas.

(RED TEZCATLIPOCA runs out from left and kneels to right of Ometeotl and Omecihuatl.)

GRANDMOTHER: The first was the Red Tezcatlipoca, god of plant life and growing things.

(BLUE TEZCATLIPOCA runs out from left and kneels to right of Ometeotl and Omecihuatl.)

GRANDMOTHER: The second was the Blue Tezcatlipoca, god of war and destruction.

(BLACK TEZCATLIPOCA runs out from left and kneels to left of Ometeotl and Omecihuatl.)

GRANDMOTHER: The third was the Black Tezcatlipoca, god of death and darkness.

(QUETZALCOATL runs out from left and kneels to left of Ometeotl and Omecihuatl.)

GRANDMOTHER: And the fourth? That was the White Tezcatlipoca, whose name was Quetzalcoatl.

(Red Tezcatlipoca, Blue Tezcatlipoca, Black Tezcatlipoca and Quetzalcoatl rise and spar with each other at down center as Ometeotl and Omecihuatl exit left.)

GRANDMOTHER: As siblings will often do, these four Tezcatlipocas fought among each other. Their battles created and destroyed the world four times.

(Black Tezcatlipoca stops fighting and faces audience.)

BLACK TEZCATLIPOCA: I, Black Tezcatlipoca, ruled the World of the First Sun! *(pulls out hand mirror)* With my magic mirror I can see into the future — and into the hearts of men!

(Quetzalcoatl mimes ramming a spear into Black Tezcatlipoca, who falls.)

BLACK TEZCATLIPOCA: My reign over the world ended when I was defeated by my brother, Quetzalcoatl!

(Red Tezcatlipoca steps forward, as Quetzalcoatl kneels.)

RED TEZCATLIPOCA: The World of the Second Sun lasted only a few centuries before Quetzalcoatl was carried off by a hurricane and, I — Red Tezcatlipoca — became ruler of the Third Sun, dominating the world with a rain of fire!

(Quetzalcoatl rises and mimes ramming a spear into Red Tezcatlipoca, who falls; Blue Tezcatlipoca steps forward, as Quetzalcoatl kneels.)

BLUE TEZCATLIPOCA: I, Blue Tezcatlipoca, ruled the Fourth Sun, in which the world was drowned by a huge flood — and all the survivors was transformed into monkeys!

(Blue Tezcatlipoca laughs wickedly as Lizard, Jaguar, Monkey, Woodpecker, Rabbit and Eagle all chatter like monkeys; Quetzalcoatl rises and mimes ramming a spear into Blue Tezcatlipoca, who falls as stage becomes quiet.)

QUETZALCOATL: And now, I — Quetzalcoatl — begin the World of the Fifth Sun!

(Animals cheer; Red Tezcatlipoca, Blue Tezcatlipoca, Black Tezcatlipoca and Quetzalcoatl exit left; as LIGHTS DIM TO HALF, Animals slowly creep to down center, except for Lizard who stays by rock.)

GRANDMOTHER: And so began the Fifth Sun, the world in which we ourselves live. During the start of this world, Quetzalcoatl re-made the human race, which had been wiped out by the other gods. Then he gave laws to the people and taught them ways to worship the gods and ancestors. But with all that he did for the world, there was still one problem — the sun itself had not returned.

JAGUAR: It is so dark! How can we live in this world where the sun never shines?

MONKEY: We might as well be flooded again!

RABBIT: Or turned into monkeys!

LIZARD: Wait! Come here! I think I see the sun behind this rock!

(Animals rush to rock.)

EAGLE: I see nothing, and my eyesight is the best of all animals!

LIZARD: But there is *something* behind this rock! I can *feel* it! Woodpecker, see if you can drill a hole!

(Woodpecker strikes rock with beak a few times. SOUND: woodpecker striking rock.)

WOODPECKER: The rock has cracked! There is a light!
MONKEY: Is it the sun?
WOODPECKER: *(peers into rock)* I cannot tell!
RABBIT: He cannot tell!
WOODPECKER: It is too small!
RABBIT: He says it is too small!
JAGUAR: Silence, Rabbit! We all have ears!
MONKEY: If it is the sun, how can we get it out?
EAGLE: We must ask Quetzalcoatl to help us. I will fly across the sky until I find him.

(LIGHTS COME UP TO THREE-QUARTERS; Eagle flaps wings and dashes offstage left.)

RABBIT: And what do we do until Eagle returns?
JAGUAR: We sing a song to honor Quetzalcoatl — *A La Vibora* — "To the Snake."

(Animals stand in three rows before rock, facing audience and sing. Jaguar and Monkey stand in front row, Rabbit and Lizard behind them in second row with Woodpecker standing alone behind Rabbit and Lizard; front two rows have their arms raised to form an arch, which the fifth animal (Woodpecker) dances through during song. At end of chorus, Woodpecker replaces Monkey, who goes to the back and repeats dancing through arches. MUSIC: "A La Víbora.")

ANIMALS: *(sing)*
A la víbora, víbora
De la mar, de lar mar
Por aquí puede pasar
La de adelante corre mucho

La de atrás se quedará
Trás, trás, trás, trás!

Manzanita de oro
Déjame pasar
Con todos mis hijos

Menos él de atrás
Trás, trás, trás, trás!

(Eagle enters from left; Animals stop dancing and singing.)

RABBIT: Look, it is Eagle!
EAGLE: And see who I have brought!

(Quetzalcoatl enters from left; Animals kneel.)

JAGUAR: The Lord Quetzalcoatl!
MONKEY: Help us find the sun!

(Quetzalcoatl steps to rock and examines it.)

QUETZALCOATL: You have yourselves found the sun. But now we must convince it to come out and light the earth.
WOODPECKER: You are a great god! You can command the sun to appear!
QUETZALCOATL: No one — god or mortal — can force the sun to act against its will.
LIZARD: Then what will you do?
QUETZALCOATL: Eagle, Monkey! Prepare my magic cloak!

(Eagle and Monkey take off Quetzalcoatl's cloak and hold it in front of him, covering him from audience view as Quetzalcoatl goes behind rock.)

JAGUAR: Quetzalcoatl has changed himself into an ant!

RABBIT: He has gone into the crack Woodpecker made in the rock!

WOODPECKER: *(peers into rock)* He is talking to the sun!

LIZARD: What does the sun say?

WOODPECKER: It says. . . it says. . . it says it wants to come out!

ANIMALS: Hurrah! Hurrah!

(LIGHTS COME UP TO FULL as Quetzalcoatl comes out from behind rock and Animals cheer.)

EAGLE: I told you Quetzalcoatl was a mighty god!

MONKEY: The mightiest of them all!

LIZARD: Let us have a fiesta!

QUETZALCOATL: Wait! The sun has agreed to come out from the rock at least half of the day. But only on condition that the creatures of the world honor him with singing and dancing.

EAGLE: We agree! We shall always honor the sun!

JAGUAR: And Quetzalcoatl, the god who found the sun!

(LIGHTS OUT CENTER AND LEFT.)

GRANDMOTHER: After awhile Quetzalcoatl built a raft of serpents and sailed into the ocean. His soul became the morning star — the planet Venus.

GRANDDAUGHTER: Has he ever come back?

GRANDMOTHER: He said that he would, and when the Spaniards came to Mexico in the 1500s, many thought it was Quetzalcoatl who had returned. But they were wrong. He has not come back — yet!

(LIGHTS UP CENTER AND LEFT. Animals and Gods at center stage singing. MUSIC: "A La Víbora.")

ALL: *(sing)*
    A la víbora, víbora
    De la mar, de lar mar
    Por aquí puede pasar
    La de adelante corre mucho

    La de atrás se quedará
    Trás, trás, trás, trás!

    Manzanita de oro
    Déjame pasar
    Con todos mis hijos

    Menos él de atrás
    Trás, trás, trás, trás!

(LIGHTS OUT.)

THE END

A La Víbora
(traditional, arranged by L.E. McCullough)

The Throne of Osiris

Ancient Egyptians believed their lives would prosper if gods and goddesses were properly worshipped. Many temples were built to conduct rituals to the deities, who eventually came to include the Egyptian kings, called Pharaohs. The great pyramids of Egypt were originally built as burial chambers for the Pharaohs and are decorated with many paintings of scenes from Egyptian mythology, mostly having to do with life after death. According to legend, when a person died, he or she had to face forty-two judges of the underworld; the deceased's heart was then weighed on a scale against the feather of the goddess Maat, who symbolized Truth and Justice. If the heart weighed more than the feather (was "heavy" with bad deeds), a monster called the Devourer of the Dead stood ready to eat the heart and condemn the person to eternal darkness.

RUNNING TIME: 15 minutes

PLACE: Egypt

CAST: 14 actors, min. 7 boys (•), 6 girls (+)

Narrator	• Seth
• Horus	+ Isis
• Ra	+ Isis as Old Woman
• Shu	+ Isis as Young Maiden
• Thoth	+ Isis as Sparrowhawk
• Geb	+ Sekhmet
+ Hathor	• Nemty

STAGE SET: large throne or chair at mid center; small 2' x 2' x 1' risers at mid left and mid right

PROPS: Nemty's ferrying pole, loaf of bread, gold ring

EFFECTS: sound — thunder and lightning

COSTUMES: deities wear ancient Egyptian garb — robes, sandals, headdresses, ankh-symbols, Egyptian-style wigs; Narrator dresses in modern Egyptian dress; Isis as Sparrowhawk wears a bird mask and wings

PRONUNCIATION:
Anubis — A-**noo'**-bis
Hathor — Ha-**thor'**
Horus — **Ho'**-rus
Isis — **I'**-sis
Khaemwese — Kem-**wes'**
Nemty — **Nem'**-tee
Osiris — O-**sy'**-rus
Ptah — (P)ta
Ramesses — **Ram'**-e-ses
Sekhmet — **Sek'**-met

Stage Plan — *The Throne of Osiris*

(SPOTLIGHT ON NARRATOR standing at down right.)

NARRATOR: *(to audience)* Greetings, my friends, and welcome to Memphis! Home of the greatest shrine to the greatest King who ever lived! What? Have I seen Elvis? *(laughs)* I am so sorry, my friends, but that is the *other* Memphis. *We* are in Memphis, *Egypt* — a city founded on the Nile River five thousand years ago as a home to the first Pharaohs of the Old Kingdom. And of all the Pharaohs of Memphis, perhaps the greatest was Ramesses the Second. Ramesses had a son called Khaemwese, who was a high priest of the Temple of Ptah. Ptah was the god of crafts; he was the power behind all of creation. And do you know how Ptah created the other gods? He thought of them in his heart and spoke their names aloud.

(LIGHTS FADE UP ON gods and goddesses standing about the stage facing the audience and forming a semicircle around the throne of Ra from mid right to mid left in this order: SHU, THOTH, ISIS, RA, GEB, HATHOR, SEKHMET. The ferryman NEMTY sits at down left, the hood of his cloak covering his head as he dozes. Shu, Thoth, Isis, Ra, Geb, Hathor and Sekhmet never turn their heads or bodies but speak only straight ahead.)

SHU: Shu — god of air! I support the sky above the earth and below the heavens!

SEKHMET: Sekhmet — lion goddess of war!

THOTH: Thoth — god of the moon and of the arts!

HATHOR: Hathor — goddess of the sky and of joy and dancing!

GEB: Geb — god of the earth! I built the foundation upon which the world rests!

ISIS: Isis — wife of mighty Osiris, the god who taught humanity the secrets of farming and civilization!

RA: Ra — god of the sun and the supreme deity of Egypt!

SHU: Once long ago, the god Osiris died in a mysterious circumstance.

ISIS: Murdered!

SEKHMET: Osiris, the first Pharaoh of Egypt, became Lord of the Underworld and ruled the Kingdom of the Dead.

HATHOR: But who was to succeed him as Pharaoh?

GEB: A bitter rivalry broke out between his brother, Seth —

(SETH trots onstage from left, flexes muscles in a pompous manner.)

THOTH: And the son of Osiris — Horus!

(HORUS trots onstage from right, bows respectfully to audience and then to deities.)

ISIS: A council of the gods was called by Ra, and the two contenders were allowed to argue their claims to the throne of Osiris.

SETH: I am the brother of Osiris. The throne should have been mine to begin with!

HORUS: You were no equal to my father! Osiris ruled wisely and gave many gifts to humanity! You bring nothing but chaos and violence to the world!

SETH: Do not listen to the wild ravings of this demented pup! He is jealous of my manly power! I propose we settle this with a battle between us — a battle to the death! And then you shall see what a hero is Seth!

ISIS: You, Seth, are a cowardly, back-stabbing murderer! You tricked Osiris at the banquet and killed him! All the universe knows it!

SETH: That is a lie!

HORUS: My mother does not lie!

SETH: This goddess must be expelled from the council!

RA: The council is not yours to command, Seth.

SETH: And until she is, I am leaving! *(exits left)*

HORUS: And I, as well! *(exits right)*

RA: What say you, council? Who shall have the throne of Osiris — Horus or Seth?

GEB: Seth has more experience. Horus is still a boy.

SHU: A boy whose father was Pharaoh!

SEKHMET: I say we let them fight it out!

THOTH: I disagree. A contest of skill would better decide.

GEB: Let them race chariots around the sun.

HATHOR: Or perform music on harp. Whoever breaks the most strings is the loser!

ISIS: Council! Where is your courage to do what is right and just? My husband was foully murdered, and you seriously talk of letting the killer have his throne?

RA: Be careful how you speak to your fellow divinities, Isis!

ISIS: And where were my fellow divinities when Osiris lay bleeding his last drops of life into the sand?

SEKHMET: Anger drips from the mouth of Isis as venom spews from a serpent. I agree with Seth — Isis should be banned from these proceedings!

THOTH, GEB, SHU, HATHOR: Agreed!

RA: It is decided. Council will meet on the island that lies north of Memphis. And Isis is forbidden to attend.

NARRATOR: But the accusations of Isis were true. Seth had killed Osiris by having a magnificent gilded chest made to exactly the Pharaoh's measurements. During the course of the banquet, Seth offered the chest to whichever guest most perfectly fit inside. When Osiris lay inside the chest, Seth sealed it with molten lead and sent it floating down the Nile, where it went out into the sea. For this evil deed, Isis swore revenge!

RA: That night the council reconvened on the island, without the presence of Isis.

GEB: But Isis had made plans of her own.

(ISIS AS OLD WOMAN enters from left holding a loaf of bread and stands above the sleeping Nemty.)

SHU: She turned herself into an old woman and approached the sacred ferryman, Nemty.

ISIS AS OLD WOMAN: Ohhhh, I am so weary! Ohhhh, I am so weak!

NEMTY: *(awakes abruptly)* Old woman! What do you want?

ISIS AS OLD WOMAN: I have brought a loaf of bread for the boy who tends cattle on the island. Will you take me across?

NEMTY: I will not! The council of the gods has ordered me to ferry no one to the island — especially not a woman!

ISIS AS OLD WOMAN: But I am just an old woman! I can give you some of this bread.

NEMTY: Bread! Hah! Go away, old woman!

ISIS AS OLD WOMAN: *(takes out golden ring)* Perhaps you would find this golden ring of more interest.

NEMTY: *(leaps up)* What an extraordinary ring! Are you going to give it to the cattle herder?

ISIS AS OLD WOMAN: I am going to give it to you, if you ferry me to the island.

NEMTY: Wellllll…all right, but tell no one. Get in the boat.

(Nemty takes up his pole and mimes poling through the water with Isis as Old Woman huddling behind him.)

NARRATOR: For taking Isis to the island, Nemty got the golden ring. But later, for disobeying the council, Nemty was punished by having his toes cut off. He declared he would never touch gold again!

NEMTY: Never!

(Isis as Old Woman exits left and Nemty stands at down left; ISIS AS YOUNG MAIDEN enters from right and crosses stealthily to down center.)

NARRATOR: When she reached the island, Isis changed her form again, this time becoming a beautiful young maiden. She came to the palace where the council was meeting and stood inside the door until Seth came along.

(Seth enters from left, notices Isis as Young Maiden, who is crying.)

SETH: What a very beautiful young maiden! But she is so sad! Maiden, what is your trouble?

ISIS AS YOUNG MAIDEN: Oh, nothing that would interest a powerful god such as you, dear sir.

SETH: But you are mistaken! I am, as you say, a powerful god — a *very* powerful god — but I am truly concerned about the plight of humanity. Tell me what worries you.

ISIS AS YOUNG MAIDEN: I am a widow of a cattle herder.

SETH: An honorable if boring profession.

ISIS AS YOUNG MAIDEN: When he died, his cattle should have passed to our only son.

SETH: That is the law.

ISIS AS YOUNG MAIDEN: But instead, a brutal stranger stole the cattle and now tells us that *he* will rule my husband's estate.

SETH: That is an outrage! The cattle should not be given to the stranger while the son is still alive.

ISIS AS YOUNG MAIDEN: Kind sir, will you help me set this matter right?

SETH: Of course I will! For it is indeed wicked for a son to be robbed of his inheritance. That interloper should be put to death!

(ISIS AS SPARROWHAWK dances onstage from left as Isis as Young Maiden dashes offstage right.)

NARRATOR: As soon as Seth spoke, Isis changed herself yet

again — this time to a sparrowhawk, who flew into the hall and addressed the council.

ISIS AS SPARROWHAWK: Seth has condemned his actions out of his own mouth! He knows it is wrong to keep Horus from the throne of Osiris!

SETH: I was tricked!

ISIS AS SPARROWHAWK: As you tricked Osiris! Let justice now be done!

RA: Council, how do you vote?

SHU: We cannot let evil rule the earth.

SEKHMET: Seth might plot to kill us as he killed his own brother.

HATHOR: Humanity deserves a better sort of ruler than Seth.

THOTH: I vote for Horus!

GEB: The throne of Osiris for Horus!

(Horus enters from right, bows to council and kneels before Ra, who stands, arms raised.)

RA: It is the will of the council of the gods that Horus be the new Pharaoh.

ISIS: The earth shall rejoice! For goodness has been restored!

SETH: And I? Horus receives the throne of Osiris! What do *I*, Seth, receive from the council?

RA: You shall be banished from the earth! You shall become thunder in the heavens and terrify mankind with your rage and bluster!

(LIGHTS FLICKER BRIEFLY; SOUND: THUNDER AND LIGHTNING OFFSTAGE; all characters freeze except Narrator.)

NARRATOR: *(to audience)* Of course, the dispute between Seth and Horus did not end but went on for centuries.

There are many myths about them, such as the time Seth tried to steal Osiris' body by turning himself into a panther but was caught by Thoth and Anubis. Ask your teachers if they will tell you the rest. In the meantime, enjoy your stay in Memphis — and watch out for those blue suede shoes!

(LIGHTS OUT.)

THE END

Tshai the Brickmaker

The roots of Chinese mythology have been traced back over 4,000 years. Chinese myths often incorporate historical kings, warriors and scholars, and worship of one's national and family ancestors is very important. The teachings of Chinese philosophers such as Confucius and Lao Tzu, as well as the Siddhartha Gautama (Buddha) of India, are also part of the mythological cycle. One ancient myth says that the world was created by Pan Gu, a child of the *yin* (dark) and *yang* (light), the two vital forces of the universe. Pan Gu grew for 18,000 years; when he died, his breath became wind and cloud, his voice thunder, his left eye the sun, his right eye the moon, his hair and whiskers the stars, and the rest of his body became mountains, rivers, plants and so forth. The alternation of night and day is when Pan Gu opens and shuts his eyes.

RUNNING TIME: 20 minutes

PLACE: China

CAST: 15 actors, min. 3 boys (•), 3 girls (+)

• Chao Po, Narrator	• Tshai the Brickmaker
3 Bricklayers	• Supreme God Jade
+ Village Girl	+ Supreme Goddess Wang Mu
Kitchen God	+ Ma-Ku, Tshai's Daughter
Soil God	2 Kuei, Demon Spirits
Doorway God	Poetry God

STAGE SET: brick kiln/throne at mid center

PROPS: 3 small bowls, broken brick, coin, stick of incense, basket

COSTUMES: characters wear Chinese robes and sandals; gods wear masks decorated with Chinese alphabet characters; Supreme God and Goddess should wear jewelry or headpiece to denote their higher status

PRONUNCIATION:
    Chao Po — Chow Po
    Kuei — Kee
    Tshai — Shy

(LIGHTS UP RIGHT on CHAO PO standing at down right; he bows and addresses audience)

CHAO PO: My name is Chao Po, a Buddhist priest of ancient China. People often ask me if the heavenly gods take any notice of the affairs of ordinary men and women. "Chao Po, Most Enlightened One," they say, "if the gods are so powerful, why do they insist on receiving the trifling sacrifices of humans? Surely what is of heaven belongs to heaven, and what is of the earth belongs to earth!" I answer them with this story of Tshai the Brickmaker.

(LIGHTS UP CENTER AND LEFT on THREE BRICK-MAKERS standing behind the kiln at mid center.)

CHAO PO: There was once a village of brickmakers in the province of Shansi. They were good brickmakers, among the best in all China. And each time before they fired the kiln to make their bricks, they gave a small sacrifice to the Kiln God.

BRICKMAKER #1: *(sets down a bowl in front of kiln, bows)* O generous Kiln God, I bring you my wife's most tasty rice cakes. May this offering please you greatly! *(bows, returns behind kiln)*

BRICKMAKER #2: *(sets down a bowl in front of kiln, bows)* Most magnificent guardian of the kiln, I implore you accept this humble homage of vegetables from my family garden. *(bows, returns behind kiln)*

BRICKMAKER #3: *(sets down a bowl in front of kiln, bows)* For your guidance in shaping the most perfect of bricks, I most sincerely offer you this bowl of chicken eggs. *(bows)* Now, fellow brickmakers, we may begin our work. Let the kiln be fired!

BRICKMAKER #1: Let the kiln be fired!

BRICKMAKER #2: Let the kiln be fired!

CHAO PO: You see, the brickmakers believed that the flames

of the kiln were fanned by the breath of the Kiln God. If the god were pleased, the bricks would be firm and well-shaped. But if were angry, he would blow a very ill wind upon the flames, and the bricks would be soft and weak.

(TSHAI THE BRICKMAKER enters from left carrying a broken brick; he stops at down center, as the Three Brickmakers turn and point.)

BRICKMAKER #1: Tshai!
BRICKMAKER #2: Tshai!
BRICKMAKER #3: Tshai!
CHAO PO: It was indeed the brickmaker Tshai! And he was beside himself with rage!
TSHAI: *(raises brick in air)* Look at this brick! It is a disgrace! Is this the best you can do for me — Tshai, the best brickmaker in all China?
BRICKMAKER #1: What arrogance! Tshai blames the Kiln God for his own poor brickmaking!
BRICKMAKER #2: Tshai is greedy! He wants to take over all the business of the village!
BRICKMAKER #3: Yet he will not offer a proper sacrifice to the Kiln God!
TSHAI: I will consult an oracle! *(to Chao Po)* You, there, priest! Come here!

(CHAO PO does not move but stares at audience.)

TSHAI: Are you deaf? I said, priest, come here!
CHAO PO: He whose language is unrestrained will have great difficulty in making himself understood.
TSHAI: Very well, you are the oracle; I shall come to you. As if I — master brickmaker Tshai — have time for silly games!

(Tshai crosses to Chao Po, who remains staring at audience.)

TSHAI: Well? Oh, but of course, you must have *your* bribe as well! *(hands Chao Po a coin)* Now, tell me what is making my bricks turn out bad?

CHAO PO: *(hands back coin)* A gift offered with disrespect yields no benefit to its giver. It is clear the god of the kiln is displeased with you, brickmaker Tshai. You have brought disharmony into the village, and you have upset the balance of the kiln.

TSHAI: Is that so? I should have known a priest would babble out such nonsense! No matter! I shall not waste my time with petty gods who hide in kilns! I shall consult the Supreme God and Goddess of the Universe — Jade and his Queen Wang Mu! They will take my side and give me power over my rivals!

(LIGHTS OUT EXCEPT FOR SPOTLIGHT on Tshai at down center [Three Brickmakers and Chao Po exit].)

TSHAI: O, Jade and Wang Mu, August Rulers of the heavens! I seek your aid in becoming the best brickmaker in the world! Hear my plea, and I will give you a great sacrifice!

(LIGHTS FLICKER, THEN COME UP CENTER on JADE and WANG MU at mid center seated on throne.)

JADE: Come, human. You seek an audience with the gods?

TSHAI: *(peers at them with uncertainty)* Is that really the Supreme God and Goddess? Or is this some sort of trick my jealous neighbors are playing upon me?

(Wang Mu extends her arm toward Tshai and snaps out

her fingers; he yells and falls to his knees as if hit by a bolt of lightning.)

TSHAI: Oww! My body is numb!

WANG MU: You wish further proof of our divinity?

TSHAI: No, no! I wish only to tell my story and receive your perfect wisdom!

WANG MU: We know your "story," human. Do not forget we know all that transpires within our earthly realms.

TSHAI: Then you will help me punish the Kiln God who has destroyed my bricks and ruined my reputation as a master brickmaker!

JADE: *(chuckles)* We will do no such thing. It is your insolence that has caused your good name to suffer.

TSHAI: *(rises)* Insolence! To a pithy god who lives in the ashes of a kiln? You must be joking!

(Wang Mu extends her arm toward Tshai and snaps out her fingers; he yells and falls to his knees.)

WANG MU: The Supreme God and Goddess do not joke!

JADE: It is clear you do not fully understand the nature of the universe, brickmaker Tshai. While my wife and I are prime rulers, we have no time to attend to every detail in creation. Therefore, we have lesser gods who take care of such business for us.

(KITCHEN GOD enters from left, dancing to down center.)

WANG MU: There is the God of the Kitchen, who watches over the cook and the preparation of healthy meals.

KITCHEN GOD: And each New Year's Eve I go to Heaven and report on the behavior of every member of the household.

TSHAI: A mere gossip!

KITCHEN GOD: To seal my lips from telling your misdeeds, you have only to offer a sacrifice of honey and sweet cakes.

TSHAI: Bribery!

(Kitchen God dances offstage right as DOORWAY GOD enters from left, crossing tiger-like to down center.)

JADE: There is the God of the Doorway, who protects the household from robbers and from pestilence.

DOORWAY GOD: I am descended from the Tiger, the fiercest of all animals! An image of me nailed to the front door of your house keeps away evil spirits!

TSHAI: A paper tiger, indeed!

(Doorway God runs offstage right as SOIL GOD enters from left, crossing to down center and miming as if sowing seed in a field.)

SOIL GOD: I am a God of the Soil, regulator of crops and harvest. The Sky God, Shang Ti, is my superior. Pray to me, and I will tell him to give you plenty of rain and sun in good mixture.

TSHAI: Your rain softens my bricks!

(Soil God walks offstage right as POETRY GOD enters from left, crossing to down center.)

POETRY GOD: And when the scholar seeks the divine muse of inspiration or the suitor seeks words to describe the beauty of his beloved, they pray to me — Kuan Ti, God of Poetry.

TSHAI: Try rhyming a brick sometime, you egghead!

(Poetry God walks offstage right as TWO KUEI, Demon Spirits, enter from left, creeping to down center as if stalking a victim; they circle Tshai, who shrinks in terror.)

TSHAI: Demons! Get away!

JADE: It is a pair of Kuei — demon spirits of the dead come back to haunt the living!

WANG MU: They drowned or committed suicide and are condemned to roam the earth as ghosts!

JADE: Sometimes they take on human form and prey upon the unwary living!

TSHAI: Save me!

WANG MU: You may save yourself, brickmaker. *(raises a stick of incense and mimes lighting it)* The Kuei are repelled by the odor of incense.

(Kuei scamper offstage shrieking right as Tshai rises and bows.)

TSHAI: Thank you, your Supremities. I see I was right to bypass the Kiln God and speak directly to the prime rulers.

JADE: And now we speak directly to *you*, brickmaker. Your wish to become the best brickmaker is granted.

TSHAI: At last!

WANG MU: But there is the matter of sacrifice.

TSHAI: Of course, of course, anything you say! A pig, a rooster, my finest sheep even! It is yours!

JADE: The sacrifice must equal the scope of your request—

WANG MU: And the degree of your disrespect to the gods.

JADE: Therefore, you will sacrifice your daughter, Ma-Ku.

TSHAI: My daughter! You are mad!

WANG MU: We are not mad. We are omnipotent.

(Wang Mu extends her arm toward Tshai and snaps out her fingers; he yells and falls to his knees as LIGHTS FLICKER AND GO BRIEFLY OUT, THEN A SPOTLIGHT COMES UP on Tshai at down center [Jade and Wang Mu exit].)

TSHAI: Sacrifice my daughter! But what else can I do? I

deserve to be the best brickmaker! But I cannot defy the Supreme God and Goddess! *(pause)* Ah-ha! I have a plan! And no spy of a Kitchen God will report this! *(exits left)*

(LIGHTS UP FULL; Chao Po stands at down right, Three Brickmakers sit at mid center, leaning against the front of kiln.)

CHAO PO: The next morning Tshai traveled to a nearby village. He found a young girl who looked very much like his own daughter, Ma-Ku, and hired her to work in his home.

(Tshai enters from left, leading a VILLAGE GIRL, carrying a basket, to down center.)

TSHAI: I must go to the kiln and prepare for the sacrifice. Tomorrow morning you will rise early and bring breakfast to the workmen.
VILLAGE GIRL: Yes, master Tshai. I will not be late.
TSHAI: After you arrive, the sacrifice will begin.
VILLAGE GIRL: I will find that most exciting, master Tshai. *(bows)*
TSHAI: You most certainly will.

(Tshai exits left; his daughter, MA-KU, enters from right and crosses to Village Girl at down center; they embrace.)

MA-KU: Hello, my new friend! My name is Ma-Ku. I am so happy my father has brought you to our house! We shall be wonderful companions!
VILLAGE GIRL: I am happy as well. But now I must sleep, for I rise early tomorrow.

MA-KU: Yes, let us sleep; the sacrifice is always a grand occasion!

(Ma-Ku and Village Girl lie down at down center and sleep; LIGHTS DIM BRIEFLY, THEN COME UP; Ma-Ku wakes and rises, picking up the basket.)

CHAO PO: But the Village Girl had worked hard that day and was very, very tired. Just before daylight, it was Ma-Ku who woke first, eager and excited about the day's celebration.

MA-KU: Sleep well, my friend. I will deliver breakfast to the workmen.

(Ma-Ku crosses to mid center and sets basket before kiln, bowing; Three Brickmakers stir and rise.)

BRICKMAKER #1: Here is the girl with our breakfast.

BRICKMAKER #2: Most excellent. Grab her and throw her in the furnace!

(Brickmaker #3 grabs Ma-Ku.)

MA-KU: Stop! What are you doing?

BRICKMAKER #3: We are making sacrifice to the Supreme God and Goddess.

BRICKMAKER #1: Tshai the Brickmaker told us the girl who brought us breakfast would be the sacrifice!

MA-KU: But he is my father!

BRICKMAKER #2: Oh, sure, he is! Nice try, Village Girl! Into the furnace!

(Brickmaker #3 pushes Ma-Ku into the kiln and over, where she falls and screams.)

MA-KU: Aaaiiieeee!

BRICKMAKER #2: Tshai will have the best bricks of all!

(Tshai enters from left and crosses to where the Village Girl still sleeps.)

CHAO PO: A short while later Tshai went to wake his daughter. When he saw the Village Girl sleeping and his daughter gone, he was seized by terror.

TSHAI: No! No, it cannot be! Ma-Ku! Ma-Ku! *(runs to kiln)* The girl! The sacrifice!

BRICKMAKER #1: Do not fear, master, we have followed your instructions to perfection.

TSHAI: But there has been a mistake! A mistake I tell you!

BRICKMAKER #2: No mistake! See, your sacrifice has already been consumed by fire.

TSHAI: No!

BRICKMAKER #3: The gods will be very pleased with your generosity, master Tshai.

(Tshai slowly walks to down center, standing behind the sleeping Village Girl, and covers his face with his hands.)

CHAO PO: Most sorrowful is the man who in deceiving others, harms only himself. For he who seeks to hide the truth, will be most surprised when he finds it.

(LIGHTS OUT.)

THE END

When a River Cries: The Myth of Oba and Oshun

It was formerly common in parts of Africa for men, especially chieftains, to marry two or more wives as part of a *patriarchal* tradition. In this ancient myth that describes the origins of two rivers in Nigeria, the goddesses Oba and Oshun were both married to the Yoruba thunder god Shango. West African mythology has spread to the New World and is found throughout South America and the Caribbean where it has combined with stories of Christian saints: Oba's legends are celebrated with those of St. Catherine; Oshun's traits are blended with Our Lady of Candlemas and Shango has been fused with St. Jerome. And in Nigeria today, the festival of Ogun is celebrated with many songs and dances honoring the Yoruba god of iron and blacksmithing.

RUNNING TIME: 15 minutes

PLACE: West Africa

CAST: 13 actors, min. 5 boys (•), 2 girls (+)

• Narrator	• Shango
+ Oba	+ Oshun
• Ogun	• Oshosi
• Obatala	6 Villagers

STAGE SET: large kettle at down center; 4' x 4' x 1' riser at mid center

PROPS: fishing pole, large kettle, *oshé* (double-headed wooden axe), ladies' hand fan, an empty bowl, broom, large iron spoon, spear, leopard-skin scarf, wine goblet, a bowl of modeling clay

MUSIC: *Oba's Wedding Song*

COSTUMES: characters wear traditional West African costumes, the Gods and Goddesses more ornate than the Narrator and Villagers; Shango can have lightning bolts embroidered on his red-and-white robe; Oshun dresses very fancy compared to Oba, with an excess of gaudy jewelry and colorful accessories

PRONUNCIATION:
  Oba — O-**ba'**
  Obatala — O-ba-**ta'**-la
  Ogun — O-**gun'**
  Oshosi — O-**sho'**-si
  Oshun — O-**shun'**
  Shango — **Shan'**-go

(LIGHTS UP FULL on NARRATOR standing at down right, holding a simple fishing pole.)

NARRATOR: *(to audience)* Greetings! Welcome to Nigeria! My name is Ibrahim, and I have spent my whole life fishing in these rivers. Is the fishing good? Oh, yes, very! But you have to be careful *where* you fish. *(points offstage left)* Do you see down there, by the bend? Yes, where the River Oba and the River Oshun meet to form one. If you listen closely, you can hear that river cry. . . yes, cry like a woman wronged and shamed. Come, I will show you.

(SIX VILLAGERS dance out from left and circle around the kettle at down center before standing on riser at mid center and singing. MUSIC: "Oba's Wedding Song.")

SIX VILLAGERS: *(sing)*
Oba, she marries Shango today!
All through the land happy people do sing her praise!
Oba, she marries Shango today!
All through the land happy people do share her joy!

(SHANGO and OBA enter from left holding hands and cross to left of kettle; in his other hand Shango carries an axe.)

VILLAGER #1: The great god Shango arrives!
VILLAGER #2: With his new wife, the goddess Oba!
SHANGO: People of the kingdom, I present to you my third wife. Is she not beautiful?
VILLAGERS #3 & #4: She is very beautiful, Lord Shango!
SHANGO: Is she not well-mannered?
VILLAGERS #5 & #6: She is very well-mannered, Lord Shango!
SHANGO: Is she not intelligent?

(OSHUN enters from right and strolls saucily up to down center, waving a hand fan.)

OSHUN: I have seen smarter goddesses in my time.

SIX VILLAGERS: *(gasp)* Aaaaahh! *(whisper)* Oshun... Oshun...Oshun.

SHANGO: *(angrily)* Oshun!

OSHUN: I may be only your second wife, Shango, but I will not be as quickly forgotten as your first.

SHANGO: Silence! I am Shango, god of thunder and lightning. *(raises axe)* With the power of my *oshé*, I punish liars, thieves and lawbreakers! How dare you speak to me in this manner, Oshun!

OSHUN: *(tickles him under chin with her fan)* Oh, husband, where is your sense of humor? *(laughs)* I have brought a present for the newest member of our household. Servant!

(Villager #1 runs up to Oba carrying a bowl; Oba looks at it, sniffs and waves it away with a grimace.)

OSHUN: It is a bowl of my special coconut yam soufflé — a favorite of our husband Shango.

SHANGO: Mmmmmm! Oshun, you are very kind. *(pulls Oba and Oshun together to join hands)* I know you wives will get along well together. Now, let the wedding feast continue!

(MUSIC: "Oba's Wedding Song" plays offstage as an instrumental as Shango leads the Six Villagers offstage left, dancing. Villager #2 re-enters and hands a broom to Oba, who begins sweeping while Oshun primps with her hair, jewelry and dress.)

OSHUN: Why, look! Lord Shango's new wife is the goddess of housework! *(laughs)*

OBA: It may surprise Lady Oshun to learn that a goddess has duties other than preening like a peacock. Her first duty is to please her husband with a clean, well-ordered household.

OSHUN: I see. And does Lady Oba feel it her duty to lecture me like a hyena pup?

OBA: I am the niece of Ogun, god of blacksmiths and all those who use iron. Ah, here is my uncle now.

(OGUN enters from left, carrying a large iron spoon, which he presents to Oba.)

OGUN: Greetings, my niece. In honor of your new marriage, I have made a set of iron cooking ware for everyone in the kingdom. *(bows, exits left carrying the broom)*

OSHUN: I was once courted by your other uncle, Oshosi — definitely the more clever of the two.

(OSHOSI enters from left, carrying a spear, and crosses to down center as if stalking game.)

OSHUN: Oshosi is the greatest hunter in the world. He would bring me the finest animal skins you could imagine!

(Oshosi takes the leopard-skin scarf from his neck and places it around Oshun's neck.)

OSHOSI: Nothing is too splendid for Lady Oshun! *(bows, exits right)*

OBA: I am not impressed by how many men you have ensnared. For I, Lady Oba, am a direct descendant of Obatala — creator of the world!

(OBATALA enters from left, followed by Villagers #2 and #3, and stands at down left. Villager #2 holds a wine

goblet; Villager #3 holds a bowl of modeling clay; Obatala fashions a figure from the clay and takes a large drink from the goblet.)

OBA: Obatala makes human beings out of clay! Every day he is hard at his task of populating the world with people.

OSHUN: And if he has had too much palm wine to drink, he creates hunchbacks and albinos! *(laughs)*

(Obatala becomes frustrated with a clay figure and smashes it up, exiting angrily left, followed by Villagers #2 and #3.)

OSHUN: I don't care how many gods you have in your family tree, Oba — they can't help you win the love of Shango.

OBA: What do you mean? Shango loves me very much!

OSHUN: Is that so? While you sweep the floor, he is out looking for wife number four.

OBA: That is impossible!

OSHUN: I know the man well, dear girl. He has broken my heart many a time. But I have something that always makes him come back.

OBA: You — you do? What is it?

OSHUN: Oh, nothing much. A smart, well-ordered goddess like you wouldn't be interested.

OBA: Oh, but I am! I am very interested!

OSHUN: Wellllll...*(rubs kettle rim with her hands)* You might say I found a secret path to his affections. *(knocks on kettle twice)*

OBA: A recipe? You have a secret recipe that makes Shango fall in love with you?

OSHUN: Sssshhhhhh...if I told you, it wouldn't be a secret.

OBA: I must know! Please, I will give you anything!

OSHUN: Now, now, dear girl. A goddess can't just throw her secrets every which way. *(takes spoon from Oba)* You just run along and sweep something. I'll cook up a fresh bowl of Shango's favorite soup.

(MUSIC: "Oba's Wedding Song" plays offstage as an instrumental as Oba exits right and Oshun begins stirring kettle; Six Villagers enter from left and cross to riser at mid center, humming "Oba's Wedding Song"; Oshun adjusts scarf as a headband that completely covers her ears.)

OSHUN: *(tastes soup)* Ahhhh, delicious!

(Oba enters from right, creeps up behind Oshun and tries to peer into kettle.)

OSHUN: *(notices Oba, shrieks)* Aiiieee! Get away, spy, get away!

OBA: But I must know! I must find a way to make Shango love me!

OSHUN: Such behavior from a goddess! Stop your begging! I will share my secret recipe with you.

OBA: Thank you, thank you!

OSHUN: Enough! Come, look.

OBA: *(peers into kettle)* That is a very strange soup.

OSHUN: Love is a very strange emotion.

OBA: What are those things floating on the surface?

OSHUN: What things?

OBA: Those big funny-shaped things that look like mushrooms.

OSHUN: Those are ears.

OBA: *(giggles)* Ears? Yes, they look like ears, in a way.

OSHUN: That is because they are.

OBA: You can't be serious!

OSHUN: Oh, but I am.

OBA: Where would anyone get ears for soup?

(Oshun adjusts the scarf tied around her ears; Oba recoils in horror.)

OBA: No!

OSHUN: I told you my recipe was a secret one.

OBA: You cut off your ears?

OSHUN: Shango is very fond of this soup.

OBA: I can't believe it!

OSHUN: And, as you know, dear girl — Shango is very fond of me, his favorite wife.

(Oba turns away and huddles as Oshun walks offstage left; after Oshun exits, Oba goes to kettle and begins stirring with spoon, taking on a demented expression.)

SIX VILLAGERS: *(murmur under Narrator)* Oba…Oba… Oba…Oba…Oba…

NARRATOR: Of course, the funny-shaped things in the soup really *were* only mushrooms. Oshun was just pretending she had cut off her ears. But Oba was desperate to win Shango's affections for herself alone.

(LIGHTS OUT; Oba screams, then silence for five seconds; LIGHTS UP FULL on Oba standing at kettle, stirring; she has a scarf tied as a headband around her ears. Shango and Oshun enter from left and cross to kettle.)

SHANGO: Ah, my young wife Oba! I hear you have been making something very special for supper.

OBA: Yes, my Lord. I have a kettle of your favorite soup.

SHANGO: Then, I must taste some!

(Oba offers him a spoonful; Shango looks at it strangely, then knocks it away.)

SHANGO: What is the meaning of this? Are you mad?
OBA: But, my Lord, I have used the secret recipe!

(Oba lifts up one side of her scarf, revealing a blood-stained patch over her missing ear.)

SIX VILLAGERS: *(gasp)* Aaaaahh! *(whisper)* Oba...Oba... Oba...
SHANGO: This woman is afflicted by demons! Take her away!

(Villagers #5 and #6 run up and grab Oba.)

OBA: But, my Lord — Oshun, she told me, she showed me! Oshun, tell him, show him!
OSHUN: Show him what?

(Oshun steps forward, taking her scarf from around her ears and revealing that her ears are perfectly fine.)

OBA: No! You tricked me! *(falls to knees)*
OSHUN: My Lord, it is clear your third wife is not as intelligent as you thought. For she has cut off her own ears and put them in your soup!
OBA: You tricked me! *(lunges for Oshun but is restrained)*

(Oshun turns and strolls to exit left.)

SHANGO: Oshun, I think you have some explaining to do as well!
OSHUN: I shall be resting by the river if you wish to visit, my Lord.
OBA: Oshun!

(Oba breaks free and chases Oshun offstage left.)

SHANGO: Oba! Oshun! Stop them! Or their fury will tear the kingdom apart! Oba! Oshun!

(Villagers #5 and #6 dash offstage left, followed by Shango calling their names.)

NARRATOR: Oba and Oshun chased each other throughout Africa for many years, until their spirits left the earth and became the rivers that bear their names today. And where the rivers meet, the water is raging and wild — just like two very jealous goddesses.

(Narrator and Villagers #1–4 sing as other characters sing offstage. MUSIC: "Oba's Wedding Song.")

ENTIRE CAST: *(sing)*
Oba, she marries Shango today!
All through the land happy people do sing her praise!
Oba, she marries Shango today!
All through the land happy people do share her joy!

(LIGHTS OUT.)

THE END

Oba's Wedding Song
(by L.E. McCullough)

♩ = 140

O- ba, she marr- ies Shan- go to- day!

La- la- la- la- la- la- la- la-

All through the land hap- py peo- ple do sing her praise!

La- la- la- la- la- la- la- la- la-

O- ba, she marr- ies Shan- go to- day!

La- la- la- la- la- la- la- la-

All through the land hap- py peo- ple do share her joy!

La- la- la- la- la- la- la

Why Bears No Longer Talk

Mythology was an important part of every aspect of life among Native American tribes. Myths explained how the universe was created, how animals and plants acquired their unique characteristics, how diseases could be cured and what one could expect in the afterlife beyond this mortal world. Divinities were not considered distant figures but were present in the here and now affecting a person's life each moment of the day. Many Native Americans undertook "vision quests," in which they created their own mythological events that were passed on to the rest of the tribe.

RUNNING TIME: 15 minutes

PLACE: Mount Shasta, California

CAST: 15 actors, min. 4 boys (•), 3 girls (+)

- • John Bright Cloud
- • Mark
- + Melanie
- • Wind Spirit
- Beaver
- Eagle

- • Sky Spirit
- + Sky Spirit's Wife
- + Sky Spirit's Daughter
- 4 Grizzly Bears
- Salmon
- Bluejay

STAGE SET: rock at down right

PROPS: map, walking stick, small piece of stick, leaves, bridal veil, tuxedo jacket, minister's collar

EFFECTS: sound — thunder and lightning; rushing wind

COSTUMES: John Bright Cloud, Mark and Melanie wear modern dress; Sky Spirit, Sky Spirit's Wife, Sky Spirit's Wife and Wind Spirit wear traditional Native American garb; Animals wear masks and body coverings

(LIGHTS UP FULL on JOHN BRIGHT CLOUD sitting on rock at down right; MARK and MELANIE enter from left and walk toward right; Mark carries a map.)

MELANIE: I think we're lost, Mark.

MARK: We can't be lost, Melanie! We're in a national park!

MELANIE: Do you know how *big* this national park is? About three million square miles!

MARK: *(consults map)* Shasta National Forest — three hundred thirty-two square miles of rugged, sweeping mountain vistas, to be exact!

MELANIE: Let's ask this man over here. Sir! Sir!

JOHN BRIGHT CLOUD: Yes?

MELANIE: Are you a park ranger?

JOHN BRIGHT CLOUD: No. I'm just a citizen enjoying the beauty of nature. John Bright Cloud is my name.

MARK: I'm Mark, and this is Melanie.

MELANIE: And we're lost! Do you know where Mount Shasta is?

JOHN BRIGHT CLOUD: I sure do. You're standing on it. The ski park is down that way.

MARK: I *knew* we weren't lost!

MELANIE: Thank you so much! We've been hiking all day.

MARK: She thought she saw a grizzly bear. Girls!

MELANIE: I did *so* see a bear! There *are* bears in California, aren't there, Mister Bright Cloud?

JOHN BRIGHT CLOUD: The bear is the official state animal of California. It's even on the state flag.

MARK: Cool! Do you go bear-hunting a lot?

JOHN BRIGHT CLOUD: Bear-hunting? I would *never* hunt a bear!

MARK: Why not? Aren't bears fierce and mean?

JOHN BRIGHT CLOUD: *(chuckles)* They are, but that's not why I don't hunt them. Sit down, and I'll tell you.

(Mark and Melanie sit; SKY SPIRIT and SKY SPIRIT'S WIFE enter from left and stand at down center. Sky

Spirit and Sky Spirit's Wife mime the action in ensuing dialogue.)

JOHN BRIGHT CLOUD: A long time ago, before there were any people on the earth, the Great Sky Spirit and his wife grew tired of their home in the Sky World, because it was so cold all the time. So they carved a big hole in the sky with a giant walking stick and pushed all the snow and ice down onto the earth below until there was a big mound that reached from the earth to the sky, nearly fifteen thousand feet high. This mound is known today as Mount Shasta.

Then the Sky Spirits walked down the mountain. Wherever they put their fingers to the ground, a tree grew. The snow melted in their footsteps, and the water became rivers. But the Sky Spirits weren't finished making things yet. Sky Spirit broke off a small piece of his giant walking stick and threw the pieces into the rivers.

(BEAVER and SALMON enter from left and dance with animal motions up stage and back down before exiting left.)

JOHN BRIGHT CLOUD: The big pieces became beaver and otter. The smaller ones turned into fish.

(Sky Spirit's Wife takes leaves from pocket and scatters them in the air.)

JOHN BRIGHT CLOUD: The Sky Spirit's Wife took leaves from the trees, threw them in the air and made the birds.

(EAGLE and BLUEJAY enter from left and dance with bird motions up stage and back down before exiting left.)

JOHN BRIGHT CLOUD: Then the Sky Spirit pointed the walking stick here and there and made all the other animals, including the grizzly bears.

(GRIZZLY BEARS #1 and #2 enter from left, walking upright, and pause at down left.)

JOHN BRIGHT CLOUD: When they were first made, the grizzly bears were covered with fur and big teeth and claws, just like now. But they could also walk on their two hind feet and talk, just like people do now.

GRIZZLY BEAR #1: Looks like rain today!

GRIZZLY BEAR #2: Yep. If it doesn't snow.

GRIZZLY BEAR #1: Think it'll snow?

GRIZZLY BEAR #2: Yep. If it doesn't rain.

(Grizzly Bears #1 and #2 exit left.)

JOHN BRIGHT CLOUD: The Sky Spirits had arranged the world pretty nice. So, they decided to live here themselves and sent for the rest of their family. The first to arrive was their eldest daughter.

(SKY SPIRIT'S DAUGHTER enters from left and sits with Sky Spirit and Sky Spirit's Wife in a semi-circle facing audience.)

JOHN BRIGHT CLOUD: The Sky Spirits made their home inside Mount Shasta. They made a big fire in the middle of the mountain and put a hole in the top so the smoke would fly out. Whenever they put a big log on the fire, the earth would tremble and sparks would shoot out the top.

(SOUND: THUNDER AND LIGHTNING OFFSTAGE, briefly then subside.)

JOHN BRIGHT CLOUD: The Sky Spirits enjoyed their new home very much. Until one day, things got a little crazy. It was the dead of winter, and the Wind Spirit sent a great storm that shook the mountain worse than anything.

(WIND SPIRIT enters dancing from left and blows and pushes wind all around; LIGHTS FLICKER ON AND OFF; SOUND: RUSHING WIND. Sky Spirits pitch and roll as if being blown about.)

JOHN BRIGHT CLOUD: The storm was so strong it blew the Sky Spirits around inside the mountain. And it blew smoke from their fire back into their eyes.

SKY SPIRIT: *(rubs eyes)* Aaauugh! This smoke is killing me!

SKY SPIRIT'S WIFE: Can't you do something about the wind?

SKY SPIRIT: It's the Wind Spirit! He's blowing too hard!

SKY SPIRIT'S WIFE: I know it's the Wind Spirit! Just make him stop, will you?

SKY SPIRIT: It's not that easy! He's hard of hearing!

SKY SPIRIT'S WIFE: Who wouldn't be, with all that wind?

SKY SPIRIT: What?

SKY SPIRIT'S WIFE: *(louder)* I said, who wouldn't be, with all that wind?

SKY SPIRIT: I *hear* you! Don't shout! *(nudges Daughter)* Climb up the smoke hole and stick your head outside. Try and get the Wind Spirit's attention.

SKY SPIRIT'S DAUGHTER: Yes, father.

SKY SPIRIT'S WIFE: And tell the Wind Spirit to not blow so hard.

SKY SPIRIT'S DAUGHTER: Yes, mother.

(LIGHTS STOP FLICKERING; Sky Spirit's Daughter stands and looks skyward, then looks at the Wind Spirit still dancing and blowing and pushing wind at down left.)

SKY SPIRIT'S DAUGHTER: I see him!

SKY SPIRIT: Wave at him!

SKY SPIRIT'S DAUGHTER: *(waves)* Hello, Wind Spirit! Hellllooooo!

SKY SPIRIT'S WIFE: Does he see you?

SKY SPIRIT'S DAUGHTER: *(waves)* Hello, Wind Spirit! Hellllooooo!

SKY SPIRIT: Be careful not to get your hair caught in the wind!

SKY SPIRIT'S WIFE: Yes, be careful, or the wind will carry you away!

JOHN BRIGHT CLOUD: The daughter was careful at first, but then she remembered her mother had once told her you could see the ocean from the top of their lodge. So, she stood up farther with her head above the smoke hole.

SKY SPIRIT'S DAUGHTER: *(peers out at audience)* The view is sooooo beautiful up here! Ooops!

(Sky Spirit's Daughter totters as if being pulled by the wind; she starts gliding toward Wind Spirit.)

SKY SPIRIT'S DAUGHTER: Help! Mother! Father! The Wind Spirit has caught my hair!

SKY SPIRIT'S WIFE: *(shakes Sky Spirit)* She's been caught by the wind!

SKY SPIRIT: *(makes futile grab for Daughter)* Wait! Tell him he can have my rivers! And all the salmon he can eat!

(Sky Spirit's Daughter falls at feet of Wind Spirit. WIND NOISE STOPS. Wind Spirit lifts arms above his head and chants.)

WIND SPIRIT: Haaaaaay-oh! The earth is shaking from the beating of my drum! Where Wind Spirit walks, all creatures fly like birds! Haaaaaay-oh! Haaaaaay-oh! *(exits left)*

(Grizzly Bears #1 and #2 enter from left and see Sky Spirit's Daughter. They help her up and brush her off, standing behind her.)

JOHN BRIGHT CLOUD: Sky Spirit's Daughter had landed many miles away at the bottom of the mountain. She was found by a pair of grizzly bears, and they raised her as part of their own family. When she grew up, she married the eldest grizzly bear son.

(GRIZZLY BEARS #3 and #4 enter from left; Grizzly Bear #3 wears a minister's collar; Grizzly Bear #4 wears a tuxedo jacket and places a bridal veil on Sky Spirit's Daughter's head.)

GRIZZLY BEAR #3: I now pronounce you Bear and Wife!
GRIZZLY BEARS #1 and #2: *(sing)* Here comes the bride! Big, fat and wide!
GRIZZLY BEAR #4: My darling! *(takes Sky Spirit's Daughter in his arms)*
JOHN BRIGHT CLOUD: And over the next few years, they had many children and lived happily. One day, though, the Sky Spirit's Daughter became lonely for her human family.
SKY SPIRIT'S DAUGHTER: I will send a vision in the form of a cloud, and ask my family to visit me here.

(Sky Spirit's Daughter mimes blowing a cloud toward her Mother and Father, who are sleeping at down center.)

SKY SPIRIT'S WIFE: *(perks up, nudges Sky Spirit)* Wake up!
SKY SPIRIT: Whhaaa! Whatizit?
SKY SPIRIT'S WIFE: There's a cloud in our room.
SKY SPIRIT: That's not a cloud, it's a vision. And our daughter is in it!
SKY SPIRIT'S DAUGHTER: Dear mother and father, it is me,

your long-lost daughter. I am living at the bottom of the mountain with many bears. Please come see me!

SKY SPIRIT'S WIFE: Bears? Did she say bears?

SKY SPIRIT: No, it was chairs! She's living with many chairs!

SKY SPIRIT'S WIFE: She married a furniture salesman?

SKY SPIRIT: Come on!

(Sky Spirit and Sky Spirit's Wife jump up and hobble over to Daughter at down left.)

JOHN BRIGHT CLOUD: The Sky Spirit and his wife ran down the mountain so fast they tore up all the ground underneath. Even today, if you look on the south slope of Mount Shasta, you can see the tracks they left in the rocks.

(Sky Spirit's Daughter, flanked by Grizzly Bears #1-4, greets her Parents.)

SKY SPIRIT'S DAUGHTER: Mother! Father! I'm so glad you could visit!

SKY SPIRIT: Daughter? Is that you?

SKY SPIRIT'S WIFE: Who are these big furry creatures in your lodge?

SKY SPIRIT'S DAUGHTER: These are my children. Your grandchildren!

SKY SPIRIT & SKY SPIRIT'S WIFE: *(gasp)* Grandchildren!

(Grizzly Bears #1-4 embrace Sky Spirit and Sky Spirit's Wife but the humans try to avoid them.)

GRIZZLY BEARS #1-4: Grandma! Grandpa!

SKY SPIRIT'S DAUGHTER: Aren't they adorable?

SKY SPIRIT: But they're a new type of creature!

SKY SPIRIT'S WIFE: Your father and I didn't make them!

SKY SPIRIT: No one is allowed to make animals except for your mother and me!

SKY SPIRIT'S DAUGHTER: But, daddy!

SKY SPIRIT'S WIFE: Don't but daddy your father, young lady! You've been *very* disobedient, making new creatures without our permission!

SKY SPIRIT'S DAUGHTER: Well, I don't care!

SKY SPIRIT: Well, you will care! Because I am going to curse these creatures!

SKY SPIRIT'S DAUGHTER: No! Please!

GRIZZLY BEAR #1: Are you nuts? Who do you spirits think you are? Gods?

SKY SPIRIT'S WIFE: We *are* gods.

SKY SPIRIT: I hereby declare that from this moment on, all of you will walk on four feet.

(Grizzly Bears #1-4 drop to ground on hands and knees.)

GRIZZLY BEAR #2: I don't like you, Grandpa!

GRIZZLY BEAR #3: Grandpa's mean!

SKY SPIRIT'S WIFE: And never again talk!

GRIZZLY BEAR #4: Grandma's mean, too!

SKY SPIRIT: And never again talk!

GRIZZLY BEAR #1: *(pause)* Neverrrrr?

SKY SPIRIT: Aaap! No more talking! I said *never!*

GRIZZLY BEAR #2: Awww, that's not fairrrrrrowwwwrrr! Rrrowwwwrrr!

GRIZZLY BEAR #3: Rrrowwwwrrr! Rrrowwwwrrr!

GRIZZLY BEARS #1-4: Rrrowwwwrrr! Rrrowwwwrrr!

SKY SPIRIT'S WIFE: And you can just stop that growling and go to your beds without any supper!

(Grizzly Bears #1-4 crawl offstage left, growling, followed by Sky Spirit's Daughter, who turns and sticks out her tongue at Parents.)

SKY SPIRIT'S WIFE: Someday you'll thank us!

SKY SPIRIT: You'd think she was brought up in a cave!

(Sky Spirit and Sky Spirit's Wife exit left after Daughter.)

MARK: And that's why you don't go bear hunting? Because bears can't talk anymore?

JOHN BRIGHT CLOUD: You haven't heard the end of the story. The Sky Spirit drove his grandchildren into the wilderness, and they scattered and wandered all over the earth. Later, they became the first people and the first Native Americans — the ancestors of all the Native American tribes.

MELANIE: And so, if you killed a bear, it would be like killing one of your relatives.

JOHN BRIGHT CLOUD: Exactly.

MARK: I've got some cousins like that. But they never *stop* talking. Even when they walk on all fours.

JOHN BRIGHT CLOUD: The sun's going down. Guess I'd better be going.

MELANIE: Thanks for the story.

MARK: And the directions.

JOHN BRIGHT CLOUD: Go in peace. *(exits right)*

(Mark and Melanie wave goodbye and walk slowly left, pausing at down center and facing audience; Grizzly Bear #1 enters, crawling, from left and stops at down left, staring at Mark and Melanie, who do not notice him.)

MELANIE: Oooh, that was some story! I've got goose bumps!

MARK: Get real, Melanie! It's just some wacko myth they make up to scare tourists! I mean, talking bears! As if!

GRIZZLY BEAR #1: Hey, kids! You wouldn't know where a fella could get a quick bite to eat around here, would you?

(Mark and Melanie freeze; LIGHTS OUT.)

THE END

The uthor

L.E. McCULLOUGH, PH.D. is a playwright, composer and ethnomusicologist whose studies in music and folklore have spanned cultures throughout the world. Formerly Assistant Director of the Indiana University School of Music at Indianapolis and a touring artist with Young Audiences, Inc., Dr. McCullough is the Administrative Director of the Humanities Theatre Group at Indiana University-Purdue University at Indianapolis. Winner of the 1995 Playwrights' Preview Productions Emerging Playwright Award for his stage play *Blues for Miss Buttercup,* he is the author of *The Complete Irish Tinwhistle Tutor, Favorite Irish Session Tunes* and *St. Patrick Was a Cajun,* three highly acclaimed music instruction books, and has performed on the soundtracks for the PBS specials *The West* and *Lewis and Clark.* Since 1991 Dr. McCullough has received 35 awards in 26 national literary competitions and had 178 poem and short story publications in 90 North American literary journals. He is a member of The Dramatists Guild, Inc. and the American Conference for Irish Studies.